Born at Tarbha in Balangir district of Orissa on May 29, 1946, Umesh Patri studied British and American Literature at the Gurukul University, Hardwar and obtained his Ph.D. from Utkal University in 1982. He is a regular contributor to periodicals and radio on various aspects of literature and religion. He won the Jibana Ranga literary award as an essayist in Oriya for 1980. At present he is actively involved in comparative literature and theology and supervises the doctoral studies. He is married and has a daughter.

HINDU SCRIPTURES
AND
AMERICAN TRANSCENDENTALISTS

Preface by Walter Harding

UMESH PATRI

HINDU SCRIPTURES AND AMERICAN TRANSCENDENTALISTS

UMESH PATRI

Intellectual Publishing House

23, Daryaganj, Ansari Road, N Delhi-110002.
(INDIA)

Sole Distributors:
Intellectual Book Corner,
23 Darya Ganj, Ansari Road,
New Delhi-110 002.

ISBN 81-7076-005-4

First edition: 1987.

Published by D.R. Chopra for Messrs Intellectual Publishing House. Composed by Sushil Singal, RB-7 Inderpuri, New Delhi and printed at Chaman Offset Printers, 1626, Suiwalan, New Delhi-2.

CONTENTS

This book is dedicated to Dr. P.C. Kar without whose encouragement, wisdom and guidance there would have been no book at all and, to the memory of my father Brindaban Patri.

SCHEME OF TRANSLITERATION

Vowels	a	ā	i	ī	u	ū	ṛ	ṝ	ḷ
	e	ai	o	au					
anusvāra	ṁ								
visarga	ḥ								
Consonant:									
gutturals	k	kh	g	gh	ṅ				
palatals	c	ch	j	jh	ñ				
cerebrals	ṭ	ṭh	ḍ	ḍh	ṇ				
dentals	t	th	d	dh	n				
labials	p	ph	b	bh	m				
semi-vowels	y	r	l	v					
sibelants	s	as in *sun*							
		ś palatal sibilant pronounced like the soft s of Russian							
		ṣ cerebral sibilant as in *shun*							
aspirate	h								

PREFACE

Henry David Thoreau, in his masterpiece *Walden*, thinking of the deep spiritual insights he had perceived in the various Indian scriptures, rejoiced, that "the pure Walden water is mingled with the sacred water of the Ganges," when American ice was shipped in his day to help cool tropical India. Fortunately, the intellectual exchange between India and the United States has continued over the years and on a far more significant level than the symbolic shipping of Walden ice to India. Just as Thoreau had been influenced by the *Bhagavad-Gitā* and other works, Mahatma Gandhi was influenced by Thoreau. And, Gandhi in turn influenced Dr. Martin Luther King. So the exchange has gone on.

Over the years some of the best scholars in both nations have studied and discussed these intellectual exchanges and their influence. Man Mohan Singh and S.P. Das in India and Frederic Ives Carpenter, Arthur Christy, and Carl T. Jackson in the United States, among others, have made notable contributions to this study. Now Dr. Patri has synthesized the work of his predecessors and added to it his own unique contributions to our knowledge.

I was deeply honoured to be asked to continue this long history of international intellectual exchange through writing a preface to Dr. Patri's book. I was delighted and honored when I was asked several years ago to be one of the official readers of his doctoral dissertation from which this book is derived. I am even more pleased now to thus greet it in its final book form.

While I find his work a particularly enlightening study of the impact of Indian thought on the American Transcendentalists (and I am especially glad that Dr. Patri, unlike some of his predecessors in the field, took care not to neglect the minor Transcendentalists, for they too have made their own special contributions, even if they have not been widely recognized), as secretary of the Thoreau Society and as one who has devoted his entire scholarly career to a study of Henry David Thoreau, I must particularly praise the depth and the profundity of Dr. Patri's chapter on the Indian influence on Thoreau. It is a masterly study.

By an odd and happy coincidence, I sit writing this introduction tonight in the very town of Concord, Massachusetts, where Thoreau and Emerson and Bronson Alcott lived out their lives and where they are now buried. Intellectually, I feel very much at home here in Concord reading Dr. Patri's work. It continues the long tradition of exchange between the two nations. And may that fine exchange continue for centuries to come.

Walter Harding
Distinguished Professor of
American Literature Emeritus
State University of New York

Concord,
Massachusetts
August 7, 1984.

ACKNOWLEDGEMENTS

I am very thankful to Walter Harding, Secretary of the Thoreau Society Inc., an eminent scholar of American Transcendentalism and an authority on Thoreau, who has kindly gone through the manuscript and given his valuable preface to my book.

I am especially thankful to the Director of American Studies Research Centre, Hyderabad, and his staff for not only giving me grants but also providing me with necessary material and facilities for the work.

My wife Prativa has constantly encouraged me in my work and has facilitated my research by doing all kinds of sundry works to give me the time I needed. My special thanks are due to her.

I would like to thank each of the following for their generosity in helping me: Dr. Vern Wagner, Dr. William Mulder, Dr. Isaac Sequeira, Dr. A.R. Rao and Dr. M.R. Satynerayan.

Lastly, I wish to express my thanks to Intellectual Publishing House for bringing out the book in a few month's time.

Umesh Patri

Akhyatrutiya 1986

I

INTRODUCTION

One of the major literary movements in America which flourished in New England, roughly from 1830 to 1860, was Transcendentalism, initiated by writers and thinkers such as Ralph Waldo Emerson, Henry David Thoreau, Amos Bronson Alcott, George Ripley, Orestes Brownson, William Henry Channing, Samuel Johnson and Moncure Daniel Conway and a few others. These writers who were members of the Transcendental Club brought into their writing a new strain that was mainly philosophical, theological, political, individualistic and at times mystical. The chief contents of their consciousness pertained to idealism, mysticism and otherworldliness. These features were, no doubt, outlandish or exotic in the background of Christianity, especially in its Protestant, Puritanic form. Some of these writers were philosophers, clergymen, poets, critics, political activists and social reformers. The major ideas that shaped the intellectual make-up of these writers were brought mostly from the Orient, especially from the Hindu and Buddhist India. The period of Transcendentalism was a period of renaissance in American thought when indigenous ideas assimilated new ideas from other cultures and enriched themselves. Never before in its history of two hundred years had America so widely opened its gate to the ancient world of the Orient.

Though the major influence, which shaped the philosophy and ideology of the Transcendentalists came from Indian religions, namely Hinduism and Buddhism, no comprehensive study was made until 1930 by any critic of the nature, magnitude and range of the Indian influence on these writers. Though a fairly large number of articles were published on Platonic, Kantian, English and French influences on Transcendentalists, only a few articles were published on Emerson's Orientalism, and these articles sought to prove that Orientalism of the Transcendentalists was chiefly Occidental in nature, without any affinity with the Indian thought. A pioneering work in this field was done only as late as 1930 by a perceptive scholar named Frederic Ives Carpenter in his *Emerson and Asia*,[1] originally a doctoral dissertation done at the University of Chicago. This book has since become a *vade mecum* of the Emerson scholars. Carpenter has demonstrated that Emerson was the first American thinker and writer to plant the Oriental, especially Indian thought, on the American soil and draw spiritual inspiration from it.

Though Carpenter initiated the study of Emerson's Orientalism for the first time, a dearth of adequate material and his lack of comprehensive knowledge of various original Indian scriptures in Sanskrit imposed severe limitations on his study. Instead of showing Emerson's deep relationship with various Indian concepts, Carpenter broadly analysed the general influence of the Orient on Emerson's writings. Though for Emerson, Asia meant predominantly India, Carpenter used Persian, Arabian and

Chinese sources in his discussion of the influence of the Orient on Emerson, thus obfuscating the line of his approach. His examination of the Oriental influence on Emerson did not take into account the complex nature of Hindu religious and philosophic texts which Emerson was familiar with. He quoted both from Emerson and Indian scriptures to elucidate his point, but he never tried to make any systematic connections between concepts like "Brahma" and "Over-soul," "Māyā" and "Illusion," "self" and "fate" etc. Whatever connections he tried to establish remained fragmentary and random. Nevertheless, his was a kind of scholarship that opened a new ground in comparative literature, and thus its strength lay in its pioneering efforts. Orient, especially India, for Emerson was a mysterious symbol, a symbol that had many complex shades of meaning. Critics and scholars took many years for a fuller exploration of the kind of influence Orient had on Emerson.

Arthur Christy's book, *The Orient in American Transcendentalism*,[2] can also be regarded as another step forward in this direction. This book is a study of Emerson's, Thoreau's and Alcott's Orientalism. It compares the spiritual concepts of Brahman, Māyā, Karma and Yoga etc. contained in the *Upaniṣads*, the *Bhagavad Gītā*, the *Haribansa* and other *Purānas*, and *Manu Samhitā* with the thought and writings of the Transcendentalists. Though this book is a commendable attempt at placing Transcendentalism in the context of Oriental thought, it lacks density and concentration in dealing with the influence of Indian scriptures on American Transcendentalists. It has digressed into Persian poetry, Sufism, Confucianism, Zoroastrianism etc.

About a decade later, Man Mohan Singh in his doctoral dissertation, "Emerson and India,"[3] discussed the familiar Indian spiritual concepts and linked them to Emerson's thought. His study is particularly interesting because it attempts to show Emerson's affinity with *Vedānta* but, like Christy's work, it lacks depth and concentration.

Taking the cue from Singh, S.P. Das in his study, "Emerson's Debt to Hindu Thought : A Reappraisal,"[4] discusses Emerson's conscious borrowings from Indian scriptures, and also suggests striking parallels between Emerson's thought and the Indian thought. His main thesis is that Emerson's writings were chiefly inspired by the Romantic, Puritan and Unitarian ideals. The similarities between Hindu thought and Emerson's writings, Das points out, are merely accidental parallelisms discernible among thinkers and philosophers. Similarities and affinities between various religions, Das concludes, are responsible for such a confusion. Critics like Carpenter, Christy and Singh who have worked on the hypothesis that Emerson was chiefly inspired by Hindu concepts and ideologies are, Das suggests, mistaken in their assumptions. Their strong emphasis on the resemblances between Hindu thought and Emerson's thought proves the influence of Hinduism on Emerson. So, Das affirms, the central concept of Emerson's thinking, the concept of "over-soul", was inspired by Christian, Neo-Plantonic, and Romantic ideals, and not by Oriental thought as is commonly assumed. He even doubts Emerson's reading of Hindu scriptures between 1830 and 1840. He writes: "There is no direct reference from Hinduism or any quotation from its scriptures to suggest Hindu borrowings in this essay,"[5] (the essay on Over-Soul).

My line of approach to the problem of borrowings and affinities is strikingly different from the line taken by Das. I would like to demonstrate that the central influence on the writings of Emerson comes from Hindu ideals and concepts. As is clear from the above discussion, none of the above writers has made a comprehensive indepth study of the precise impact of Indian concepts underlying Hinduism, Buddhism and Vedānta on the writings of Important Transcendentalists. Again, none of the writers discussed above has pointed out the precise sources in Hindu scriptures which have influenced Emerson and others. Also, these scholars have not been able to show a philosophic system existing in the transcendentalists, especially in Emerson, which is very close to the Hindu philosophical system.

The purpose of this study, therefore, is to take off from where others have left, discover new sources and interpret them in a new way. A clarification of my objective is warranted here. In dealing with the Transcendentalists, the main emphasis, as has been said, would be on Hindu and Buddhist influences not on Mohammedan, Sufi, and Chinese influences. I would like to suggest here that Transcendentalism owes a great deal to Indian scriptures without which it would not have been what it was.

[II]

Transcendentalism, as we know, is both a philosophical tradition and was an American intellectual movement in the nineteenth century. In philosophy, the concept of Transcendentalism goes back to Plato (427- 347 B.C.) in the Western tradition and to the rise of speculative philosophy in the *Upaniṣads* in India. The American Transcendentalism is a significant literary and philosophical movement confined to the New England States in the nineteenth century. Until the nineteenth century, thinkers and writers in America looked towards European ideas and borrowed them freely. With the emergence of Transcendentalism a new phase in American intellectual life came into being. A new group of writers and intellectuals formed a compact circle in Boston and ushered in the Transcendental movement having clearly defined principles. In an anonymous pamphlet, "An Essay on Transcendentalism," published in 1842 the principles of Transcendentalism were laid down in the following manner: "Transcendentalism.... maintains that man has ideas, that come not through the five senses, or the powers of reasoning; but are either the result of direct revelation from God, his immediate inspiration, or his immanent presence in the spiritual world," (and) "it asserts that man has something besides the body of flesh, a spiritual body, with senses to perceive what is true, and right and beautiful, and a natural love for these, as the body for its food."[6] The cause of Transcendentalism was championed chiefly by Emerson and supported by his colleagues. It was he who "scouted the trail that the others were to follow?"[7] Its chief source, as I shall discuss later, was the Orient, especially India. Its immediate intellectual reason for turning its attention on the Orient was dissatisfaction with the intellectual and spiritual life of America. Carl T. Jackson remarks: "A combination of factors contributed to the favourable transcendentalist response to Oriental thought. Intellectually, its spokesmen were ripe for new ideas. In rebellion against the Calvinistic Christianity, rationalistic Unitarianism, and materialistic Lockeanism that then dominated New England intellectual life, leading members of the movement were receptive to the new currents of idealism they found in the Orient."[8]

Introduction

The chief source of Transcendentalism in the West was Plato's concept of intuition. The Neo-Platonist like Plotinus and other religious mystics in the same line also influenced the movement. But the Oriental concepts, primarily the Hindu concepts, which the Transcendentalists borrowed and assimilated into their own system of thought, enriched their philosophy and gave it a dynamic orientation.

The Transcendentalists in America dealt with the fundamental issues of human life such as the nature of the Universe, the nature of man and his place in the Universe, the nature of good and evil, and man's duty to himself and to his fellow beings. It was, in its immediate context, a reaction against the excessive rationalism of the eighteenth century, and in this sense it was characterised by a soaring idealism. It was also, broadly speaking, a part of the Romantic movement that started almost all over the West in the nineteenth century. Its immediate source was Coleridge and the English intuitionists, and partly the German idealists like Kant, Schelling, Fichte, Jacobi. It interpreted reality in terms of idealism and romanticism and opposed all types of materialism and industrialism. In another aspect, Transcendentalism emphasized a return to nature somewhat in a Rousseaustic vein. It saw in nature a manifestation of the Supreme Spirit of the Universe. This pantheistic aspect inherent in Transcendentalism is akin to the Hindu thought in which the animate as well as the inanimate are part of a cosmic scheme operated by an overseeing God. Transcendentalism saw in science and technology a sinister force that destroys nature and finally engulfs man. Hence the opposition to railways and factories which were destroying the landscape and upsetting the ecological balance. It embodied an organic worldview which was opposed to the mechanistic clock-work concept of the Newtonian Universe. Nature was held by the Transcendentalists to possess an Immanent divinity. Transcendentalism was also a revolt against John Locke's empiricism, materialism and sensationalism. John Locke's sensationalism dominated the American philosophical scene for more than a century and it was expanding through Unitarian philosophy. Locke's empiricism did not believe in the innate and the *a priori* aspects of the human mind. This view was rejected by the idealism of the Transcendentalists. The concept of Over-Soul also played an important role in the worldview of the Transcendentalists. Though Transcendentalism flourished in the New England atmosphere of Christian orthodoxy and puritanism, it nevertheless opposed many of the basic tenets of Christianity. It believed in the potentiality of human nature and rejected the idea of guilt associated with the idea of original sin. It also opposed the Puritanic denial of life based on arid asceticism in favour of a healthy enjoyment of life in the midst of nature. These various aspects of Transcendentalism are inextricably connected with the mystical tradition of the Orient, chiefly embodied in Hinduism and Buddhism.

The concept of pantheism, inherent in Transcendentalism, is basically a Hindu concept. In the *Īśa Upaniṣad*, the universe is conceived as a manifestation of God, *Īśavāsyam idam̄ sarvam yet kiṁ ca Jagatyam Jagat*.[9] In the entire universe whatever is matter or spirit is the divine manifestation of God. Emerson writes in a similar vein: "The world proceeds from the same spirit as the body of man. It is a remoter and inferior incarnation of God, a projection of God in the unconscious."[10] An important corollary of pantheistic belief is that everything in the phenomenal world including man, is a miniature universe, a microcosmos or *imago Mundi*. This idea, present in many cultures, is subscribed to by the Transcendentalists. When the Transcendentalist says, "The world globes itself in a drop of dew," he is voicing the old microcosmic idea. The *Vedas* and the *Upaniṣads* contain the earliest concept of microcosm implied in the phrase, *Atmo Sarvosmi*. The central idea of the *Upaniṣads* is that all is present in each and each is present in all. This concept was fundamental to the Transcendentalists.

Besides pantheism, mysticism is another aspect which is common to both the Transcendentalists and ancient Indian thinkers. Christians described mysticism as a union with God or a spiritual marriage with the deity. In Hinduism, Buddhism and Taoism mysticism is more or less described as an egoless state in which the person experiences the totality or the wholeness of the Universe. In this experience, "the soul seem to go beyond the body and to achieve identification with God: the individual transcends the limits of his individuality and feels himself part of the whole....."[11] All dualistic categories disappear and the person experiences *Samādhi, Nirvāṇa* or a state of bliss. Dr. Radhakamal Mukherjee in his book *The Theory and Art of Mysticism*, describes mysticism in its higher forms as: "the experience of an eternal mode of existence which transcends space and time, and in which a final and complete unification is postulated...."[12]

The experience is also pantheistic in nature in which the experience of God in all and all in God is produced. The mystic in such a state feels that "the universe is not a "creation distinct from God ..... God is the universe, and the universe is God."[13] *The Maṇḍukya Upaniṣad* emphasizes this point saying that all is Brahman.

The Transcendentalists like Emerson, Thoreau and Alcott were all disposed towards mysticism at one time or other and had the mystical experience. Carpenter is of opinion that Emerson was not a mystic, like other sages, but merely a theoretical mystic who believed in the doctrine that "God, or the ultimate nature of reality, may be known in an immediate apprehension or insight,"[14] without experiencing the self-surrender of a practising mystic. But this observation can easily be refuted in the face of many available evidences that Emerson had the spiritual experience on more than one occasion. In the beginning of *Nature* (1836), his earliest work, Emerson describes ascetic experience which is in a very true sense mystical. Recounting his experience he writes: "Standing on the bare ground, - - my head bathed by the blithe air and uplifted into infinite space, - - all mean egotism vanishes. I became a transparent eyeball; I am nothing; I see all; the currents of the Universal Being circulate through me; I am part or parcel of God. The name of the nearest friend sounds then foreign and accidental: to be brothers, to be acquaintances, master - or servant, is then a trifle and a disturbance."[15]

The above experience demonstrates that his everyday personality, his ego is dissolved and he is merged into the universe and has an experience of the totality of existence. In another place, Emerson speaks like a sage who had the awareness of the Divine. He writes: "A certain wandering light comes to me which I instantly perceive to be *the cause of causes*."[16] (Italics mine.) In 1864, he lamented that due to old age he was having that vision only rarely and asked: "Can we attend those enlargement and that intellectual e'lan which was a daily gift."[17] Not only these, there are many other expressions of such experience in poems like

"Brahma" and "Hamatreya," essays like "Illusion" and "Over-Soul" which describe mystical experience of a very high order. Therefore, Carpenter's view that Emerson's interest in mysticism was merely theoretical is not acceptable.

Professor Rudolph Otto, whom Carpenter quotes approvingly, observes that Eastern mysticism is "static" and Western mysticism "dynamic,"[18] perhaps because of the Eastern emphasis on quietism and passivity and the Western emphasis on dynamism. But mysticism, as we have noted earlier, has universal characteristics and cannot be divided into such polar divisions and watertight compartments. Though there are evidences that Emerson disapproved of quietism (and so also Thoreau,) the experience he had attained was led to by the metaphysical thinking done mostly in the light of Indian idealism and German Transcendentalism. In him verily" .... the twain do meet in the sympathies of the mystical bond, which is universal."[19] For Emerson, God was not a superhuman personal God but a state of consciousness and an absolute principle underlying the "Spiritual structure of the Universe." William James remarks that "Emersonianism ..... seems to let God evaporate into abstract Ideality."[20] Hence Emerson's experience, described in the passage quoted above, is akin to the experience of totality or the experience of the Brahman propounded in Vedāntic mysticism. Emerson had a contemplative mind as opposed to the general Western ideal of activity. Though it is very difficult to say whether Emerson arrived at a mystic union with God or "an ineffable communion with the Over-Soul,"[21] one can conclude by browsing through his various passages that "his whole mental and spiritual attitude was mystical."[22] It was a mysticism of a purer kind where the emphasis was on experience and not simply on theory. Christy is of the opinion that "Emersonian thought was a matter of almost pure mysticism."[23] He goes on to say that "The plain man's *Weltanschauung* is artless and non-speculative, based on commonsense. That of Emerson, Thoreau, and Alcott was the fruit of the mystical temperament and some metaphysical thinking, mixed with an unusual dash of the urbane."[24]

Though Emerson was disposed towards mysticism he nevertheless remained pragmatic and a Yankee realist; and as a practical man he took active interest in the activities of everyday social transaction. His closest companion, Thoreau, was a greater realist and a pragmatist than Emerson, although he too, like, Emerson, was mystically oriented. Thoreau was, no doubt, a mystic, but of a different order. The influence of Indian scriptures and attitude to life worked on him in a different way than they worked on Emerson. The influence of Indian philosophical thought made Thoreau an idealist, a hermit and a recluse. It made him a Yogi, or strictly speaking, a *Karma Yogi*. The period of his study of Oriental scriptures in general and Hindu scriptures in particular was briefer than Emerson's but his response to Hindu scriptures was of a general nature and intellectual in character. He was more attracted, as Carl T. Jackson suggests, to "the mystical sweetness and the strange resonance of Oriental thought, to Oriental symbols and images more than to Oriental ideas."[25] His encounter with Hindu scriptures was brief, but intense. In Jackson's view, "Thoreau perhaps dived more deeply than Emerson into the waters of Oriental thought but he revealed less interest in exploring its secrets and surfaced more quickly."[26] But even then he was inspired by some of the ideas of Hindu philosophy and way of life. He was attracted by the asceticism of Indian sages and their cultivation of self-discipline and detachment as a means of self-realization. One of the important phases of the Indian scheme of life is *Vanāprastha* or retirement to the forest for leading a spiritual life untrammeled by the fetters of the world or *Samsāra*. Thoreau undertook an experiment in this line when he retired to the Walden Pond. Though he was chastized by R.L. Stevenson who called him a "Skulker"[27] for his shirking social responsibility and retiring to the Walden Pond, his action could be justified in the light of the Indian ethos of detachment and escape from material desires.

Thoreau's action can be justified in view of his philosophy of life which he developed quite early in life, the philosophy of leading a detached, self-controlled, and selfless life. The monk or the sage, according to both the Indian and the Western monastic tradition, is a "marginal person," an outsider, and not a person in the established order of society. He is an outsider in a very real sense. Such a person is bound to be looked down upon by society as a "Skulker." The man who listens to inner dictates of the soul is bound to come in to conflict with society.

Thoreau was a mystic in the sense of a Yogi or a detached person, though there are a fewer passages in his writing than we find in Emerson or Alcott in which immediate mystical experiences have been described. B.V. Crawford, writing about what Thoreau learnt from India, says: "Two aspects of Transcendentalism were especially significant to Thoreau. The first was the stress which it laid upon solitary communion with the infinite."[28] In 1838, when Thoreau was reading the *Illiad* he recorded his mystical experience in the unfinished essay, "The Sound and Silence": "She (Silence) is audible to all men, at all times, in all places Grecian, or silent and melodious, Era is ever sounding in the ears of men. A good book is the plectrum with which our silent lyres are struck Silence. She cannot be done into English .... Nevertheless we will go on."[29]

But the most important passage that comes closer to Emerson is to be found in the beginning of "Solitude" in *Walden*. There one finds an ecstatic experience which verges on the mystical. The passage is: "This is a delicious evening, when the whole body is one sense, and imbibes delight through every pore. I go and come with a strange liberty in Nature, a part of herself. As I walk along the stony shore of the pond in my shirt-sleeves, though it is cool as well as cloudy and windy, and I see nothing special to attract me, all the elements are unusually congenial to me. The bullfrogs trump to usher in the night, and the note of the whippoorwill is borne on the rippling wind from over the water. Sympathy with the fluttering alder and poplar leaves almost takes away my breath; yet, like the lake, my serenity is rippled but not ruffled. These small waves raised by the evening wind are as remote from storm as the smooth reflecting surface. Though it is now dark, the wind still blows and roars in the wood, the waves still dash, and some creatures lull the rest with their notes. The repose is never complete. The wildest animals do not repose, but seek their prey now; the fox, and skunk, the rabbit, now roam the fields and woods without fear. They are Nature's watchmen,- links which connect the days of animated life."[30]

A.B. Alcott, another member of the Transcendental group, was first introduced to Oriental scriptures after he met Emerson. He continued to be a close friend of Emerson and was more mystically - oriented than Thoreau. A true embodiment of the Transcendental spirit, he showed a deep interest in Oriental scriptures. His passionate interest in Hindu scriptures inspired him to read and teach the *Bhagavad Gitā*. He writes: "I dine and pass the afternoon with the Adams and read *Bhagavad Gitā* to a large audience in the evening, with lively discussions, etc."[31] Till the end of his life, as Christy says, he ".... continued to work as educator and promulgator of mystic love, but gradually his labour became less personal and centered around his administrative duties as dean of the Concord Summer School of Philosophy."[32]

[III]

In the foregoing pages we have seen from internal evidences from texts that the Indian and Transcendentalist thoughts were almost alike in subjects like pantheism, mysticism and idealism. The external evidences, now available, suggest that the Transcendentalists actually read and were influenced by some Indian scriptures. F.I. Carpenter remarks: "To Emerson's mind Hindu philosophy expressed the essence of Orientalism. Often he identified the whole Orient with it. When speaking vaguely of *Asia*, he was usually thinking of Hindustan."[33] More than any other Transcendentalist, Emerson was influenced by Indian scriptures the most. His initial rebellion against Christianity in its various forms prompted him to find a ready refuge in the idealism of Hinduism. It opened a new vista and a window for him which remained with him till the end of his life. Essentially his temperament was that of a Hindu and Brahmin, a fact which has been accepted by many Hindu scholars. In the memorial symposium, *The Genius and Character of Emerson*, published after Emerson's death Protap Chunder Mazoomdar calls Emerson: "... the best of Brahmans."[34] He again remarks: "Amidst this ceaseless, sleepless din and clash of Western materialism, this heat and restless energy, the character of Emerson shines upon India serene as the evening star. He seems to some of us to have been a geographical mistake. He ought to have been born in India. Perhaps Hindoos were closer kinsmen to him than his own nation because every typical Hindoo is a child of Nature."[35]

Emerson himself had felt this spiritual inclination and affinity towards the Hindus. He received so much from India that throughout his writings he admitted his indebtedness to Indian thought in unambiguous terms. For him the idealism of the Hindus propounded in the *Upaniṣads*, the *Bhagavat Gitā* and other Indian scriptures, was based on fundamental concepts. He turned Eastward towards India very early in life, when he was in his teens. The year 1820 may well be regarded as the beginning of his interest in the Orient. He was introduced to Orientalism by his loving aunt Mary Moody Emerson who sent him, "A Hymn to Nārāyena"[36] by Sir William Jones. Emerson copied a portion of the poem in his diary and wrote a few sentences by way of comment, a fact which shows his early interest in Orientalism. After reading this, Emerson was very much moved by its thought content and wrote back to his aunt on June 10, 1822: "I am curious to read your Hindu mythologies. One is apt to lament over indolence and ignorance, when we read some of those sanguine students of the Eastern antiquities, who seem to think that all the books of knowledge, and all the wisdom of Europe twice told, lie hidden in the treasures of the Brahmins ...."[37]

During the next decade or so, Emerson's interest in Orientalism grew steadily and became more sharply defined. He read a large number of extracts including excerpts from *Mahābhārata* [his reference to sage Vyasa spelt as "Viasa" is significant] from various Indian philosophical books and, according to Man Mohan Singh's account, he read about nineteen articles on India published in *Edinburgh Review* during the period 1821.[38] In fact, he had no opportunity to read any complete, full-length Hindu scriptures till 1836, the year in which he read the *Code of Manu*, translated by William Jones. In the same year his famous book *Nature*, which contains the salient idea of Indian idealism, was published. We may mention here that Emerson and his colleagues had no knowledge of Sanskrit which prevented them from reading the Hindu scriptures in original. For their reading, they had to depend on whatever English translations were available then. Arrival of a translation of Indian scripture in Boston was, therefore, news for the Transcendentalists and always brought a breath of fresh air to them. The English translations of Indian texts were made mostly by the efforts of the Asiatic Society of Bengal, and translators of these texts were such persons as Sir William Jones, Henry Thomas Colebroke, Sir Charles Wilkins, Horace Hayman Wilson and Brian Houghton Hodgoson. Emerson read *Vedas*, a few Buddhist scriptures, Veeshnu Sarma's *Heetopades* and most importantly the *Bhagavad Gitā* which he first mistook for a Buddhist scripture. Writing to Elizabeth Hore in 1845 he says: "The only other event is the arrival in Concord of the *Bhagavad Geeta*, the much renowned book of Buddhism"[?][39] (Emerson, in the beginning, it ought to be noted, took *Bhagavad Gitā* to be a Buddhist scripture.)

Before reading the full text of the *Bhagavad Gitā* Emerson had some idea of it most probably from Victor Cousin's lectures entitled *Cours de L'histoire de la Philosophie* translated by H.G. Linberg in April 1828. Emerson acknowledged his first acquaintance with the *Bhagavat Gitā* in a letter written to William Emerson on May 24, 1831.[40] Afterwards he read the whole text of the *Bhagavat Gitā* which was the greatest single influence on him. He wrote: "I owed,-- my friend and I,-- owed a magnificent day to the *Bhagavat Geeta*. It was the first of books; it was as if an empire spoke to us, nothing small or unworthy but large, serene, consistent, the voice of an old intelligence which in another age and climate had pondered and thus disposed of the same questions which exercise us."[41] The central concept of his philosophy, the concept of Over-Soul, in all probability, is conceived by his reading of the *Bhagavad Gitā* where the Supreme Spirit is called *Ādhyātaman* or *Paramātman*.[42] Over-Soul seems to be a literal translation of these two words. Emerson deals with the concept of immortality of the soul in his essays, "Immortality" and "Illusion."

The other Hindu concepts which profoundly influenced Emerson were the concepts of *Māyā, Fate and Law of Karma, Rebirth, Transmigration of Soul*, transcendence and immanence of Divinity, pantheism, mystic description of the ultimate reality embedded in the Upaniṣadic method *Neti, Neti* (not this, not this). Of these the idea of "neti" is an important one which influenced Emerson most. The nature of ultimate reality which is infinite cannot be grasped by the mind which is finite and limited. The mind can only operate in the field of the known. Therefore, the process of arriving at the ultimate reality involves the denial of whatever is known by the mind and is regarded in ignorance as the ultimate reality. By discarding the false categories one after another (through Neti Neti...,) one may eventually reach the highest state which is that of no-mind. This approach, through negation, is at the very heart of *Vedānta*.

Like the concept of "Neti," the concept of "Māyā" or illusion has influenced Emerson a great deal. 'Māyā' means that Brahman is the ultimate reality and the phenomenal world is not ultimately real or, in other words, has no *Pāramarthika sattā*. The word "māyā" is translated as "illusion" which is not to be confused with "delusion." This is a very old Hindu concept referring to the creation of all manifest things from ignorance (*avidyā*,) through the two processes: 1. Veiling (*āvarana*) the reality; 2. building on the basis of the veiling by projection (*vikshepa*). When a rope is taken not to be a rope it is called veiling, and when the rope is erroneously taken for a snake it is the projection (*vikshepa*) of *Māyā*. This is later embodied in Sankara's well-known verse: *Brahma Satya Jagan mithyā jiva Brahmaiva nāpara* or Brahman is the truth and the world is illusion, and the individual self is the part of the Brahman. (Trans. mine.) Emerson in two of his poems "Illusion" and "Māyā" hinted at the above Hindu concept: The following passage from "Maia" demonstrates this idea:

> Illusion works impenetrable,
> Weaving webs innumerable,
> Her gay pictures never fail,
> Crowds each on other, veil on veil,
> Charmer who will be believed
> By man who thirsts to be deceived.[43]

In 1861, he wrote in his *Journals* about the Māyā of Vishnu.[44] In another context, he said that the world is born of Māyā.[45] The poem "Hamatraya" also seems to have been influenced by the concept of Māyā where the difference between "I and You" or "Mine and Yours"[46] has been regarded as ignorance. In fact, there are a good many passages in his *Journals* and essays which demonstrate that he had a comprehensive conception of the Hindu idea of *Māyā*. In his essay, "Illusion," for example, he writes: "I find men victims of illusion in all parts of life. Children, youths, adults and old men, all are led by one bauble or another. Yoganidra, the godess of illusion, Proteus or Momus, or Gylfi's Mocking,-for the Power has many names,-is stronger than the Titans, stronger than Apollo."[47] The affinity between Emerson's concept of Māyā and Vedāntic concept of Māyā is so close that one is inclined to disagree with Das when he says that the concept of Māyā was influenced by a concept in the Bible.[48]

The Hindu concept of 'niyati,' which means fatality or destiny, is another concept which Emerson has discussed in many contexts. Fate is also called *daiva* since it is part of the divine law given effect by gods. It implies an inexplicable as well as inexorable decree which human beings are forced to accept. Fate, truly understood, is the effect of past *karma* (action) which must happen. In the *Bhagavad Gitā* Sri Krishna tells Arjuna: "None can ever remain really actionless even for a moment; for everyone is helplessly driven to action by the Gunas, born of Prakriti."[49] Emerson accepts the law of *Karma* in general but does not seem to accept the deterministic aspect of the above concept. This kind of disagreement suggests that he had properly understood the concept. He wrote in one of his journal entries: "As long as I am weak, I shall talk of Fate; whenever the God fills me with his fulness, I shall see the disappearance of Fate."[50] His essay "Fate" also contains his negative attitude. His attitude to fate was influenced by Hindu, Greek and Mahammadian ideas. Emerson's reading of the *Code of Manu* enabled him to share this fundamental Hindu belief. The logic involved in the law of *Karma* aroused in him great appreciation. The doctrine of compensation, discussed in his essay "Compensation," bears ample evidence of this. Emerson's support of the Law of *Karma* in its central aspects has been criticised by many for its anti-Christian stance, but Emerson understood the simple logic involved in the law that 'whatever you sow, so shall you reap'. The Hindoos asserted this logic by saying that all human sufferings had their origin in *Prārbdha Karma*, which means deeds of one's past life. Suffering in this life is only the immediate and perceptible fruit (*phala*) of action in another life as well in this life. Like the Hindoos, Emerson also believed in rebirth and transmigration of soul.

The doctrine of rebirth is a necessary ccrollary to the law of *Karma* and an important Hindu and Buddhist concept, which assumes that living beings including human beings undergo a series of incarnations, rebirths. These constitute a cycle which comes to an end only when one realizes the ultimate reality or, as the Buddhists say, one's Buddha nature. If one does not reach the goal in one life, there is always another chance. There is no eternal damnation if one cannot reach the goal in one life. As *Bhagavad Gitā* puts it, a man who has fallen from Yoga due to some fault on his part is born again with better opportunity and more congenial environment:

Prāpya puṇyakṛtāṁ Lokān
Uṣitvā Śāśvaatīḥ Samāḥ
ścīnāṁ śrīmatāṁ gehe
yogabhraṣṭo bhijāyate.

(Having attained to the worlds of the righteous and having lived there for

> countless years, he who falls from yoga is reborn in the house of the pure and prosperous.)[51]

The doctrine of rebirth also implies that if a man does evil deeds, he may have a nonhuman body in his next life.

The idea of rebirth or reincarnation is found throughout Emerson's works and journals. He writes: "The transmigration of souls is no fable...."[52] Faith in transmigration of souls, though antithetical to Christianity, appealed to him because it countered the notion of finality inherent in Christianity, and embodied a vision of correction through successive stages of development until one achieves beatitude and divine bliss.

Some scholars are of the opinion that Emerson had independently, or through influences other than the Orient, had formed and developed these concepts into which the Hindu concepts were subsequently assimilated. Carl T. Jackson, for instance, subscribes to such a view. He remarks: "Of course, he (Emerson) had already arrived at these concepts before developing a wide and sympathetic interest in the Orient, but it is evident that he quickly assimilated the Hindu formulations into his thought."[53] But, as I have shown by quoting external evidences, Emerson developed these concepts after reading Indian scriptures without which he could not have developed his concepts clearly. If India's influence on Emerson was intellectual and philosophical in nature, it was practical and pragmatic on Thoreau. Emerson was a thinker and a philosopher, whereas Thoreau being a practical man was more interested in the application of ideas in his daily life. Thoreau, unlike Emerson, had no knowledge of Indian scriptures during his youth. It was only in 1837 that he was initiated into Indian scriptures and literature while living in Emerson's house as a handyman. The first significant Hindu scripture that he read, during 1841-1842 was Sir William Jones' translation of the *Law of Manu*. He recorded his impressions in a journal on May 31, 1841: "That, title, 'The Law of Manu with the Gloss of Culluca,' Comes to me with such a volume of sound as if it had swept unobstructed over the plains of Hindostan; and when my eye rests on yonder birches, or the sun in the water, or the shadows of the trees, it seems to signify the laws of them all. They are the laws of you and me, a fragrance wafted down from those old times, and no more to be refuted than the wind. When my imagination travels eastward and backward to those remote years of the gods, I seem to draw near to the habitation of the morning, and the dawn at length has a place. I remember the book as an hour before sunrise."[54]

There are many instances in his writings which suggest that he was ecstatic after reading Indian literature. The important and oft-quoted entry in his *Journal* reads: "I cannot read a sentence in the book of the Hindoos without being elevated as upon the table-land of the Ghauts. It has such a rhythm as the winds of desert, such a tide as the Ganges, and seems as superior to criticism as the Himmaleh mounts."[55] After reading the *Vedas*, he was so overjoyed that he wrote: "One wise sentence (from the Vedas) is worth the state of Massachusettes many times over."[56] This impassioned statement may appear somewhat exaggerated, but it ought to be borne in mind that it was the spontaneous reaction of the poet and a mystic who had discovered a new terrain of human mind in the rich literature of the Orient.

The most important book which influenced him was the *Bhagavad Gitā* which he read in

Charles Wilkins English translation. He wrote in his first book, *A Week on the* Concord and *Merrimack Rivers*, his reaction thus: "The Bhagavat-Geeta is less sententious and poetic, perhaps, but still more wonderful, sustained and developed. Its sanity and sublimity have impressed the minds even of soldiers and merchants.... To the practical they will be common sense, and to the wise wisdom; as either the traveller may wet his lips, or an army may fill its water-casks at a full stream."[57]

Gita's doctrine of *anāsakta* or non-attachment, its idealism of retirement to solitude *vivikta savi laghynasi* altered his lifestyle and thinking profoundly. The doctrine of non-attachment is central to the teaching of the *Bhagavad Gitā*, an aspect which Thoreau cultivated throughout his life.

Thus, it can be said in conclusion that Transcendentalism in America was strengthened by such writers as Emerson, Thoreau, Alcott etc. who accepted various ideas from different cultures and made them their own. Of the ideas that enriched this intellectual movement, the philosophical and religious ideas from ancient India were the most prominent, without which Transcendentalism would not have got its vitality and strength.

Footnotes:

1. Frederic Ives Carpenter, *Emerson and Asia* (1930; rpt. New York: Haskell House, 1968).

2. Arthur Christy, *The Orient in American Transcendentalism* (1932; rpt. New York: Octagon Books, 1963).

3. Man Mohan Singh, "Emerson and India," Diss. Univ. of Pennsylvania 1946.

4. S.P. Das, "Emerson's Debt to Hindu Thought: A Reappraisal", Diss. Gurunanak Univ., Amritsar, India, 1977.

5. Das, p. 91.

6. This anonymous pamphlet probably written by Charles Mayo Ellis, (1818-1878), "An Essay on Transcendentalism," quoted by W. Harding, "Transcendentalism," *Encyclopaedia Americana*, 1965 ed., p.3.

7. Carl T. Jackson, "Oriental Ideas in American Thought," in *Dictionary of the History of Ideas*, ed. Philip P. Wiener (New York: Charles Scribner's, 1973), III, p. 429.

8. Ibid.

9. S. Radhakrishnan, trans., *The Principal Upaniṣads* (1953 rpt. London: George Allen and Unwin, 1968), p. 567. (Īsa Upaniṣad, I)

10. Emerson, *Complete Works of Ralph Waldo Emerson* (1865; rpt. Boston and New York: Houghton, Mifflin and Co., 1903), I, pp.64-65. (Nature).

11. F.I. Carpenter, *Emerson Handbook* (New York: Handricks House, 1953), p. 118.

12. Radhakamal Mukerjee, *The Theory and Art of Mysticism* (Bombay: Asia Publishing House 1960), p. 41.

13. W.T. Stace quoting Prof. Abraham Wolf from Encyclopaedia Britannica in *Mysticism and Philosophy* (Philadelphia and New York: J.B. Lippincott Co., 1960), p. 208.

14. *Emerson Handbook*, p. 114.

15. *Complete Works*, I, p. 10. (Nature)

16. Emerson, *Journals of Ralph Waldo Emerson* ed. E.W. Emerson and W.E. Forbes (Boston and New York: Houghton Mifflin, 1909-14), IV, 248-249.

17. Ibid., X, 47.

18. *Emerson Handbook*, p.115.

19. Christy, *The Orient*, p. 271.

20. William James, *The Varieties of Religious Experience* (New York: The Modern Library, 1902), p.32.

21. P.F. Quin, "Emerson and Mysticism," *American Literature*, XXI (Jan., 1950), 399.

22. Leyla Goren, "Elements of Brahminism in Transcendentalism of Emerson," *The Emerson Society Quarterly*, 34(1 qtr. 1964), 8.

23. Christy, *The Orient*, p. 266.

24. Ibid. p. 267.

25. Jackson, p. 431.

26. Ibid.

27. R.L. Stevenson, "Henry David Thoreau: His Character and Opinion," in *Thoreau: A Century of Criticism*, ed. Walter Roy Harding (Dallas: Southern Methodist Univ. Press, 1954), p.59.

28. B.V. Crawford, *Henry David Thoreau* (New York: American Book Co., 1934), p.XXIX.

29. Thoreau, *Writings of Henry David Thoreau* ed. Bradford Torrey (1906; rpt. New York: Ams Press, 1968), *Journal* VII, pp. 64, 67-69.

30. *Writings*, II, p.143. (Walden).

31. Alcott, Manuscript Journals, see: Christy, *The Orient*, p.325.

32. Ibid., p. 258.

33. Carpenter, *Emerson and Asia*, p.103.

34. Protap Chunder Mozoomdar, "Emerson as Seen from India," in *Concord Harvest*, ed. K.W. Cameron (Hartford: Transcendental Books, 1970), p. 187.

35. Mozoomdar, p. 186.

36. Sir William Jones, trans. "A Hymn to Narayena," *American Transcendental Quarterly*, I. No. 20 (Fall, 1973), pp.578-583.

37. Emerson, *The Letters of Ralph Waldo Emerson*, ed. Ralph L. Rusk (1939; rpt., New York and London: Columbia Univ. Press, 1966), I, pp. 116-117.

38. Singh, p. 26.

39. *Letters*, III, p. 290.

40. Ibid., I, pp. 322-323.

41. *Journals*, VII, 511.

42. Swami Chidbhavanand, trans., *The Bhagavad Gitā* (1965; rpt. Madras: Sri Ramkrishna Tapovanam, 1969), 8:2, p. 452.

43. *Complete Works*, IX, p. 348. (Maia).

44. *Journals*, IX, 302.

45. Ibid., X, 159.

46. *Complete, Works*, IX, p.36. (Hamatreya).

47. Ibid., VI, p.313. (Illusions).

48. Das, p. 277.

49. *Bhagavad Gitā*, 3:5, p. 215.

50. *Journals*, VI, 189, see also 317; VII, 8.

51. *Bhagavad Gitā*, 6:41, pp. 403-404.

52. *Complete Works*, II, p.32. (History).

53. Jackson, p. 430.

54. Journal, I, P. 261.

55. Ibid., p. 266.

56. Ibid., II, p. 4.

57. *Writings*, 1, pp. 153-154 (A Week).

II
BRIDGING THE GULF

This chapter is an exposition of a crucial phenomenon, namely the nature and the scale of the cultural link between the Indian subcontinent, or South Asia in general, and the American continent from the middle of the late paleolithic age to the time of Transcendentalism. It suggests a continuity of that link so that the Transcendental movement can be put in proper perspective. The hypothesis behind such a study is that Transcendentalism is not an isolated phenomenon and can be linked to the past and present of the American interest in India. Contact with India through culture, religion, trade and commerce was there long before the present interest in India grew. There is a missing link in history between the extinction of pre-Columbian civilization of American Indians, especially the Mayans, Aztecs and Incas, and the establishment of European civilization in the new continent in the sixteenth and seventeenth centuries after the discovery of America by Christopher Columbus in 1498 and Vespucci Amerigo in 1507.

The West, despite its materialism and technology, has always been eager to accept new forms of spiritual experience and enlightenment from the East. Though India's early influence on many countries in Asia and Europe has been an established fact, the exact nature of her influence on America in the days of antiquity has been a controversial issue. The American tribes such as Mayans, Aztecs and Incas, who developed a very high civilization long before America was colonised by Europeans, supposedly migrated from India and South East Asia between 20,000 and 40,000 years ago. The above tribes observed caste distinctions, developed a priesthood, wore sacred threads and ear-rings, had an artisan class who produced objects of great artistic merit, and developed knowledge which was almost scientific in character. It is generally believed that Indians who are closer to the Mongoloid race crossed the Pacific and came to America by way of the Behring Strait in several groups over a long period and populated the American continent. This migration, it is believed, stopped many centuries before the arrival of Columbus in the New World.[1]

These features, which are similar to the features of Indian castes, suggest that India influenced these civilizations. Heine Geldern remarks: "There is no doubt that a simple and unbiased comparative analysis of Aztec and Mayan religions will uncover many characteristics of ancient Buddhist or Hindu influences, or of both. To give but one example: the conception of hell and of the punishments inflicted upon sinners is so similar to those of Buddhist and Hindu beliefs in both outline and detail, that one is led inescapably to postulate an historical relationship."[2]

After the civilization of Mayans, Aztecs and Incas became extinct, there was a blank period in history until large-scale migration of European settlers into America started in the sixteenth century. The American Indians belonging to various tribal groups, who lived as aboriginal tribes in America then, did not transmit their Indian culture to the new settlers. The influence of India, therefore, came through new sources.

America remained a British colony from 1606 to 1776. During the colonial period, contact between India and America was very little, and whatever contact was made it was through Britain. It was only after the American independence that worthwhile and direct contact was established between India and the USA. It started with trade, missionary and other intellectual activities on a very small scale, and in the past two centuries it has grown steadily. Since the eighteenth century, ideas have been flowing back and forth between the two countries. For the Americans, after independence, India was apparently a country of mystery and wonder, full of strange customs and superstitions. Before Emerson began to take serious interest in India, the richness of India's culture and profundity of her philosophy were not fully recognized. After America became independent in 1776, cultural contact between India and America slowly began to grow. It first started through trade and commerce between the two countries. The first American ship named *United States* reached the Madras port in 1784. A Bengali businessman, Ram Doolal Dey, helped a great deal in promoting trade between India and America. Ships from America began to come to Calcutta port, and contacts between the two countries grew further. Apart from fostering trade and commerce, these contacts gradually turned into cultural interactions. Before the advent of Transcendentalism, the ground was prepared, particularly in Boston, for ushering in a new climate of sensibility with India occupying a conspicuous place.

There is an interesting episode about the Indo-American trade. In 1833, an imaginative American youngman named Frederick Tudor sent to Calcutta an astonishing cargo consisting of tons of ice cut from the ponds of New England. The ship, *Tuscany*, that carried ice to Calcutta was the first ship carrying ice to India, enabling the communities in Calcutta to have cold drinks. A part of the shipment of ice was taken from the Walden pond, and Thoreau, who lived nearby, was amused at this and rhapsodized: "...the people of India and America drank water from the same well."[3] During the early period of the Indo-American trade, Indian goods also created in USA an interest in Indian art.

The contact of the American merchants with Indian people contributed significantly to the growth of American interest in India. The common curiosity regarding Oriental people, their costumes, their way of life gave rise to an interest among intellectuals in Indian philosophy and literature. By 1790s, the visiting merchants carried books from Calcutta printing presses for their friends at home. It is interesting to note that in 1812 when Captain Heard of Salem came to Calcutta he was requested by his friend Henry Pickering to obtain for him a copy of the "Sanskrit Bible." He perhaps received, as J.T. Reid surmises, a copy of Wilkins' translation of the *Bhagabad Geeta*. By "Sanskrit Bible," Pickering might have meant the sacred book of the Hindus comparable to the Bible of the Christians.[4] To give another example, a learned Unitarian clergyman of Salem Reverend William Bentley requested the captain of a ship that was in trade with East India to fetch him copies of books dealing with India. The *Christian Register* of April 21, 1827 records that a file of Bengal Periodicals called *Hur Karu* was received "by the politeness of a gentleman in the *Mars* from Calcutta."[5] During the hey-day of the Indian trade a young man named Charles Eliot Norton (1827-1908), who worked in his uncle's counting house that was handling Indian trade befriended many Indian intellectuals and Rajas during his many visits to India and thereby helped in strengthening New England's cultural contact with this country. Thus, before the Transcendentalists came, the cultural link between the two countries had already been established.

Besides trade and commerce, activities of the missionaries in India, brought India and America closer and laid the infrastructure for the Indo-American cultural and philosophical link. Though missionary activities were sometimes viewed with suspicion, they served a very useful purpose, when the Christian missionaries became interested in Hindu and Buddhist scriptures. Some of the missionaries translated them into English and took them home for American intellectuals. Some of the missionaries did constructive work in India and helped in furthering understanding between the two nations. The Americans are truly proud of their activities in India. Stephen B.L. Penrose remarks: "American contacts with Indians have been strong in the missionary field. Some of the greatest figures in the Protestant church have devoted their lives to the betterment of the people of India, and have done much to create in America goodwill towards India. Such men as R. Stanley Jones, the Apostle of Indian Road, and Sam Higginbottam, beloved agriculturist, have been, unofficial, two-way ambassadors between India and the American people, and their books have exerted considerable influence on public opinion in America. There is a strong reservoir of friendliness towards India in America, and in India towards America, which is a monument to the work of generations of missionaries."[6]

Most probably the first American missionary interest in India was evinced by a famous American divine, Reverend Cotton Mather, who in 1710 wrote to a Danish missionary in Malabar, India: "What has been done by the Dutch Missionaries at Ceylon and what is being done by the Danish missionaries at Malabar; one would think, might animate us to imitate them!"[7] Unlike the other Christian missionaries, the American missionaries in India are noted for their educational and medical work rather than evangelical work. It ought to be borne in mind that unlike Britain and France America had no colonial interest in India. The aim of American missionaries was mostly humanitarian, altruistic, and at times evangelical. The *Boston Magazine* of that early period shows that the Americans were mostly interested in famine, epidemic, superstitions and war in India.[8] It was the Unitarians who actually were responsible for bridging the gulf between India and America through their two-way acculturation work. Whatever little cross-cultural contact had been established between India and America by the early traders was consolidated and strengthened by the missionaries. The Unitarians discovered early that an inter-relationship could be developed between a few educated Indians and themselves as there was a common doctrinal ground. It was Raja Rammohun Roy and the members of his Brahmo Samaj which attracted the attention of the Unitarian ministers in New England. Spencer Lavan writes: "Even through the misunderstandings and excessive expectations each side had from the other, something dynamic occurred which demonstrated an openness between Unitarians and Brahmos not experienced by Indians in any earlier encounter with missionaries and seldom encountered in any later experience."[9]

The Indian connection of the Unitarians is significant because of their close links with the Transcendentalists of New England. The Transcendentalists came to know India through their Unitarian friends. William Adam, the Unitarian minister who served in India, was a close friend of Rammohun Roy and both of them collaborated to produce a new translation of *The New Testament*. Adam studied Sanskrit and Bengali and worked in Calcutta as a journalist. After his return to Boston in 1838, he delivered a famous lecture, "On the Life and Labours of Rammohun Roy".[10] He met Emerson sometime in 1839 and told him about Roy's activities in India. Emerson records this meeting in one of his letters.[11] William Adam was mostly responsible in familiarising the Boston intellectuals with Rammohun Roy's reform movements. His lecture on Roy inspired some Transcendentalists to take greater interest in Hindu thought and religious doctrines. Emerson was, of course, aware of Roy's movement before Adam told him about it, but Adam renewed his interest in India through first-hand information. *The North American Review*, started in 1815, published two articles on India: one was William Tudor's "Theology of the Hindoos as taught by Ram Mohun Roy"[12] and the other, an article of general nature by Theophilus Parsons entitled, "Manners and Customs of India."[13] Emerson's early contact with India was made by his reading of this journal along with *Christian Observer* of London which also discussed religious activities in India, especially those of Rammohun Roy. As early as 1810 *The North American Review* published a detailed analysis of Roy's translations of Hindu literature.[14] Adrienne Moore had furnished a comprehensive list of American journals which discussed

Rammohun Roy's life and writings.[15] The *Christian Register* alone mentioned in its various issues his name 136 times.[16] All these facts undoubtedly demonstrate that Rammohun Roy was singularly responsible for creating the American interest in India then.

Another Unitarian minister, Charles Dall, who later joined the Brahmo Samaj was also responsible for bringing Hindu and Brahmo ideas closer to the Bostonians. However, Dall's thinking was not closer to the Emerson-Parker Transcendentalist vision; his was closer to the W.E. Channing's (a minor Transcendentalist) tradition.

The trade and missionary activities that brought India and America closer together laid the foundation for deeper intellectual activities which reached their height in the 1840s with the Transcendentalists. Sir William Jones, the founder of the Asiatic Society of Bengal, did pioneering work by translating the *Laws of Manu* and Kalidasa's *Sakuntalā*. These books along with the translation of Jaydev's *Gitagovinda* were known to the Concordians immediately after their publication. The Massachusettes Historical Society was founded in 1791, and four years later, in January 27, 1795, it elected William Jones as a corresponding member and wrote to him thus: "Your character, and the attention which the world allows you to have paid to learning have induced us to pursue such measures as we hope will obtain your good wishes."[17] Though the letter did not reach Jones before his death, liaison between the Massachusettes Historical Society and the Asiatic Society of Bengal was established. Richard Watson, a professor of Divinity during the time wrote to Archdeacon of Ely on May 9-10, 1780: "Since the recognised antiquity of the available Indian annals seemed to militate against the Mosaic history, and since 'the Gento scriptures' made 'no mention of the deluge' and since the 'Bramins' affirmed that the deluge never took place in 'Indostan,' was it not important for Christian scholars to translate all the Indian scriptures and, if possible, find the corroboration they desired?"[18]

Another important association of this period, the Anthology Club, tried vigorously to bring knowledge about India to American people. In its two journals, *Monthly Anthology* and *Boston Review*, articles on India and translation of Indian works were frequently published. The most notable publication in it was the Act One of Sir William Jones's translation of Kalidasa's *Sakuntalā* [or *The Fatal Ring*]. Kalidasa, regarded as the Oriental Shakespeare, was first published in America in the *Monthly Anthology*.[19] In fact, *Sakuntalā* earned the prestige of being the first work of a Hindu author published in the USA. The Harvard University promoted this kind of cultural link by introducing Sanskrit in its curriculum, a rare distinction, no doubt, in those days. In 1811, David Irving of Edinburgh presented to Harvard College Library a copy of Thomas Brown's *The Renovation of India a Poem* alongwith *The Prophecy of the Ganges, an Ode*.[20] An early Sanskrit scholar Fitzedward Hall (1825-1901) who was a student at Harvard University in 1846 came to India in search of his fugitive brother and eventually studied Sanskrit alongwith a few other Indian languages. He later became a professor in Sanskrit and English at the Government College of Banaras. He also had the distinction of becoming the first American Indologist to edit the Sanskrit text, *Vishnu Purāna*. He also contributed a number of popular articles on India to an American journal called *Lippincutt's Magazine*.

The first notable American Sanskrit scholar was Edward Elbridge Salisbury (1814-1901) who taught a few students at Yale University during the heyday of Transcendentalism. The scholarly band of students he taught did a lot of serious work in Indology. Of them William Dwight Whitney, who can be rightly regarded as the father of Indology in the USA, did the most significant work. His authentic edition of *Atharva Veda* was a significant contribution to the Indo-American cultural link.

The Transcendentalists were thus brought up and nourished in an atmosphere charged with knowledge and familiarity with Indian scriptures, and a blending of Indian and American cultures. They developed an eclectic attitude to life. The three major contemporaries of Emerson, Edgar Allan Poe (1809-1849), Herman Melville (1819-1891) and Walt Whitman (1819-1892) who were to a considerable extent influenced by Transcendentalism, were also influenced by Indian philosophy. Though consciously an anti-Transcendentalist, Poe has used some ideas of Transcendentalism as well as the philosophy inherent in the *Upaniṣads* and the *Bhagavad Gitā* in his famous prose work *Eureka*. *Eureka* appeared in 1848 and eleven years later Sarah Helen Whitman wrote: "It has been said that his (Poe's) theory, as expressed in 'Eureka,' of the Universal diffusion of Deity in and through all things, is identical with the Brahminical faith as expressed in the Bhagavat Gitā."[21] One of the central ideas in the essay is self-diffusion of God in the creation, though according to the Christian belief God created the Universe standing apart from his creation. Poe says that God "passes his Eternity in perpetual variation of Concentrated Self and almost Infinite Self-Diffusion. What you call The Universe is but his present expansive existence."[22] That the universe is an "expansive existence" of the creator has been the central doctrine of the Hindu cosmogenesis. God is supposed to have created the universe out of Himself and He has Himself become the indwelling spirit of every atom in the phenomenal world. The first line of *Īsaponisad* reads thus: *Īsāvāsyamidaṁ sarvaṁ yetkiṁca jagatyāṁ jagat.* ("All this whatever moves in this moving world, is enveloped by God. Therefore find your enjoyment in renunciation...")[23] The following verse from *Taittirīya Upaniṣad* also agrees with Poe's theory of creation: "Let me become many, let me be born. He performed austerity. Having performed austerity he created all this, whatever is here. Having created it, into it, indeed, he entered."[24] Also, about the dissolution of the universe, Poe holds a view similar to the Hindu concept of *Pralaya*. He writes: "The final globe of globes will instantaneously disappear, and ...God will remain all in all."[25] Hindoos believe that there will always be a fresh creation after each dissolution which will again be followed by another creation in a cyclic pattern. Poe also believes in this kind of cyclic pattern in creation. In his own words: "... another action and reaction of the Divine will."... "a novel Universe swelling into existence, and then subsiding into nothingness, at every throb of the Heart Divine?"[26] Towards the end of his essays one finds a profound vision of Soul or *Atman* and God or *Brahman* which looks as though the lines have been lifted from the pages of the *Upaniṣads*. "No thinking being lives who, at some luminous point of his life of thought, has not felt himself lost amid the surges of futile efforts at understanding or believing, that anything exists *greater than his own* soul... that no one soul *is* inferior to another--that nothing is, or can be superior to any one soul that each soul is, in part, its own God."[27] The identity of the soul and God or the individual self and the *Brahman* is the essence of the teaching of *Vedānta*.

Though Poe appears at times opposed to Transcendentalism, there are many instances in this essay which clearly show his indebtedness to Emerson. Poe's essay has been compared to Emerson's *Nature*.[28] There is a clear relationship between Emerson's concept of the primal unity of the universe pervaded by Over-soul, and Poe's concept of the unity of the universe. Arnold Smithline remarks: "In his assertion of the unity of man and the cosmos, and of reliance upon intuition as the best means of realizing that ultimate Truth, Poe is following the main tenets of the Transcendentalists."[29]

Like Poe, Herman Melville, it is assumed by some critics, was also influenced by Hindu mythology. Though during his round-the-world tours he never visited India, he was keenly interested in Indian lore, a fact which is evidenced in the discussion between Melville and the poet Oliver Wendell Holmes. The following passage suggests this fact: "At length, somehow, the conversation drifted to past Indian religions and mythologies, and soon there arose a discussion between Holmes and Melville, which was conducted with the most amazing skill and brilliancy on both sides. It lasted for hours...."[30] Besides, there are evidences to show that he had read W.J. Mickle's essay, "Inquiry into the Religious Tenets and Philosophy of the Brahmins," Thomas Maurice's *Indian Antiquities* and an article on "Hindu Superstitions" in Chambers' *Miscellany of Useful and* entertaining *Knowledge*.[31] *Moby Dick* contains a large number of references to Hindu imagery and symbolism. The central symbol of *Moby Dick*, the white whale, may have been forged out of his knowledge of Indian mythology, particularly the concept of *Matsya Avatāra* of Vishnu. Vishnu, the chief God of the Hindu pantheon, was born as a fish in one of his incarnations. H.B. Kulkarni, in his book *Moby Dick: A Hindu Avatar: A Study of Hindu Myth and Thought*,[32] has made a detailed analysis of the parallels between Melville's concept of the white whale and Vishnu's incarnation as a fish. In the chapter "Monstrous Pictures of Whales" in *Moby Dick*, Melville refers to the concept of Matsya avatar: "Now, by all odds, the most ancient extant portrait anyway purporting to be the Whale's, is to be found in the famous cavern-pagoda of Elephanta, in India. The Brahmins maintain that in the almost endless sculptures of that immemorial pagoda, all the trades and pursuits, every conceivable avocation of man,were prefigured ages before any of them actually came into being. No wonder then that, in some sort, our noble profession of whaling should have been there shadowed forth. The Hindoo whale referred to, occurs in a separate department of the wall, depicting the incarnation of Vishnu in the form of Leviathan, learnedly known as the Matse Avatar."[33]

The reference to Elephanta caves in the passage is, undoubtedly, based on a confusion of sources. In Elephanta caves there is no representation of Vishnu as a fish or whale. Melville must have seen the picture of *Matsya Avatāra* in Thomas Maurice's *Indian Antiquities*, and as Howard P. Vincent observes he "got it mixed up in hasty recollection with an account of Elephanta in the same volume."[34] Melville also makes a similar confusion in his concept of "Dark Hindu half of nature" referred to in *Moby Dick*, suggesting that the dark side of the world is essentially a Hindu view of the world. Despite these conceptual errors, the fact remains that Melville was acquainted with Indian mythologies and employed them wherever he found them interesting and appropriate to developing his own concepts. The concept of Vishnu's ten incarnations has been used in a satirical vein in *The Confidence Man*, a novel dealing with how one person in ten different guises plays a confidence game with passengers in the boats in the Mississippi in order to swindle them.

The influence of Indian scriptures on Walt Whitman has been an established fact. His *Leaves of Grass* deals with concepts which are typically Hindu. There are several ideas in *Leaves of Grass* which are identical with the ideas of *Advaita Vedānta* and its source books such as the *Upaniṣads* and the *Bhagavad Gitā*. In 1856, shortly after the publication of *Leaves of Grass*, Thoreau greeted Whitman saying that the book was "wonderfully like the Orientals."[35] Malcolm Cowley remarks that, "Most of the Whitman's doctrines, though by no means all of them, belong to the mainstream of Indian Philosophy."[36] S. Radhakrishnan has categorically affirmed the Indian inspiration behind Whitman's writings: "Whitman turns to the East in his anxiety to escape from the complexities of civilization and the bewilderments of a baffled intellectualism."[37] Emerson himself thought that *Leaves of Grass* very much resembled the *Bhagavad Gitā*, "a mixture of the *Bhagavad Gitā* and the *New York Herald*."[38] The concept of the *Atman* (individual self) merging into the *Brahman* (the world self,) the concept of transfiguration and several other concepts, basic to Indian thought, are employed by Whitman in poems like "Song of Myself," "A Passage to India" etc. Although Whitman denies having read the *Bhagavad Gitā* before the publication of *Leaves of Grass*, there are strong grounds to disbelieve him. His personal copy of the *Bhagavad Gitā* was a translation by Cockborn Thomson, which was presented to him as a Christmas gift by an Englishman Thomas Dixon in

1875, after the publication of *Leaves of Grass*, but one can assume that Whitman may have been familiar with the Indian text before he was presented with one by his English friend. Although Whitman may not have read the *Bhagavad Gitā* before writing *Leaves of Grass*, he had a sound knowledge of Vedic literature, a fact corroborated by Dorothy F. Mercer when she says that there is a great similarity between Whitman's prose and Sanskrit prose in general.[39] What she implies is that the literary atmosphere during the 1840s and 1850s, being charged with Hindu philosophy, must have unconsciously influenced Whitman's thinking: "It was in this atmosphere, impregnated with interest in Hindu philosophy, literature, and religion that Whitman reached manhood."[40] Emerson might also have been a potent influence on him. In 1847, Whitman reviewed Emerson's "Spiritual Laws" and subsequently underwent a spiritual transformation, which might have been due to the indirect influence of Indian thought filtered through Emerson's writings. Whitman expressed his gratitude to Emerson for his transformation saying: "I was simmering, simmering, simmering, Emerson brought me to a boil."[41] Whitman may also have been interested in Yoga. O.K. Nambiar[42] claims that in section 5 of the "Song of Myself" Whitman had sudden burst of psychophysical energy which is very akin to the unfolding of the energy hidden in *Kundalini*, the serpent power that lies coiled at the base of the spinal column and flowers when there is some spiritual progress in the Yogic lines. "Song of Myself" describes the experience of unitive life which is possible on the part of a person whose hidden and potent energy has bloomed.

Another nineteenth century poet and a contemporary of Emerson, John Greenleaf Whittier (1807-1892) was influenced both by Indian philosophy and the Transcendentalism of Emerson.

In 1852, Emerson lent him a copy of the *Bhagavad Gitā* which presumably inspired him. The impression he had about the *Bhagavad Gitā* is recorded in a letter written to Emerson: "I will even keep it until I restore it to thee personally in exchange for Geo[rge] Fox [The founder of the Society of Friends, or Quakers.] It is a wonderful book -- and has greatly excited my curiosity to know more of the religious literature of the East."[43] He was stimulated by books like Edwin Arnold's *The Light of Asia*, Alger's *The Poetry of the Orient* and Max Muller's *Sacred Books of the East*. He also read Kendersley's *Specimens of the Hindu Theatre* and was familiar with the *Journal of the Asiatic Society of Bengal*. Arthur Christy is of the opinion that he offered in his "poetic work more poems on Oriental themes, more paraphrases of Oriental maxims and more imitations of Oriental models than may be found in Emerson's verse..."[44] Poems like "Miriam," "The Preacher," "The Over Heart," and "The Brewing of Soma" etc. deal specifically with Indian themes. The concept of 'Over-Heart' is very close to Emerson's concept of Over-Soul. Both are translations of the Hindu term *Adhyātman*. He was interested in the Brahmo Samaj and translated a few of its hymns. In the introduction, he writes thus: "I have attempted this paraphrase of the Hymns of the Brahmo Samaj of India, as I find them in Mozoomdar's account of the devotional exercises of that remarkable religious development which has attracted far less attention and sympathy from the Christian world than it deserves, as a fresh revelation of the direct action of the Divine Spirit upon the human heart."[45]

Thus, to sum up, before Transcendentalism developed as a powerful intellectual movement, the climate was already ripe for it. The gulf that existed between India and America was bridged by Christian missionaries, Orientalists, traders, travellers, and scholars. Once the bridge was made, the flow of traffic between India and America began to increase. The momentum which the Transcendentalists gave to the cultural links between the two countries became stronger. The Christian Science Movement of Mrs. Mary Baker Eddy, the New-humanism of Babbitt and Paul Elmore More, the New Transcendentalism movement of the Beat Generation and various other cults which arose as a result of continuing interest in Indian culture, philosophy, religion and way of life carried forward the work of the Transcendentalists with greater vigour and zeal. Now India is no longer considered as a country of mystery and superstitions, ungraspable and inaccessible to Americans; its culture and religious heritage have been the source of endless debate and discussion. What the Transcendentalists achieved on a rudimentary scale has been realized fully in the twentieth century.

Footnotes:

1. See Walter Gardine, "Asiatic Influences on Pre-Columbian Cultures," trans. Rosanna Rowland, *Diogenes*, 87 (Fall, 1974), p.106-125.

2. R.H. Geldern, "Challenge to Isolationists," in *Hindu America*, by Chaman Lal (Delhi, Chaman Lal, 1966), Intro. p.x.

3. G. Bhagat, *Americans in India: 1784-1860* (New York: New York Univ. Press, 1970), p.107.

4. John T. Reid, *Indian Influences in American Literature and Thought* (New Delhi: Indian Council for Cultural Relations, 1965), p. 7-8.

5. Ibid., p. 8.

6. Stephen B.L. Penrose, Jr., and Oliver J. Caldwell, "Ties that Bind," in *The Asian Legacy and American Life*, ed. Arthur E. Christy (1942; rpt. New York: Greenwood Press, 1968), p.128.

7. Mukhtar Ali Isani, "Cotton Mather and the Orient", *The New England Quarterly*, 43 (March 1970), p.54.

8. J.P. Rao Rayapati, *Early American Interest in Vedanta* (Bombay: Asia Publishing House, 1973), p.80.

9. Spencer Lavan, *Unitarians and India: A Study in Encounter and Response* (Beacon Press: A Skinner House Book, 1977), p.3.

10. Lavan, p.51.

11. *Letters*, II, p.201.

12. William Tudor, "Theology of the Hindoos as Taught by Ram Mohan Roy," *The North American Review*, VI (1817-1818), 386-393.

13. Theophilus Persons, "Manners and Customs of India," *The North American Review*, IX (1819), 36-58.

14. Reid, p. 16.

15. Rao Rayapati, p.90.

16. Ibid.

17. K.W. Cameron, "Indian Superstition By Ralph Waldo Emerson," *The Emerson Society Quarterly*, 32, I (III Qtr., 1963), p.3.

18. Ibid., p.6.

19. Ibid.

20. Ibid., p.7.

21. Sarah Helen Whitman, *Edgar Poe and His Critics* (1859; rpt. New York: Rudd and Carleton, 1860), p. 65-66.

22. Edgar Allan Poe, *The Works of Edgar Allan Poe*, ed., Intro., E. Markham (New York and London: Funk and Wagnalls, 1904), IX, p.154. (Eureka).

23. *Principal Upanisads*, p 567.(Īśa Upaniṣads,I)

24. Ibid., p. 548 (Taittiriya Upaniṣad, 11:6)

25. *Works*, IX, p. 150. (Eureka).

26. Ibid., p. 151

27. Ibid., p. 152-153

28. Patrick F. Quinn, "Poe's *Eureka* and Emerson's *Nature*," *Emerson Society Quarterly*, 31 (II Qtr., 1963), 4-7.

29. Arnold Smithlin, "*Eureka*: Poe as Transcendentalist," *Emerson Society Quarterly*, 39 (II Qtr., 1965), 28.

30. M.B. Field, *Memories of Men and Some Women*, quoted by James Baird, *Ishmael* (Baltimore: Johns Hopkins Press, 1956), p.176.

31. Reid, p. 53.

32. H.B. Kulkarni, *Moby-Dick: A Hindu Avatar: A Study of Hindu Myth and Thought* (Utah: Utah State Univ. Press, 1970).

33. Herman Melville, *Moby Dick: or the White Whale* (New York: Harper and Brothers, 1950), LV, p. 292.

34. Howard P. Vinunt, *The Trying-out of Moby Dick*, quoted by Reid, p. 53.

35. Malcolm Cowley, Introduction to Walt Whitman's *Leaves of Grass: The First (1855) Edition* (1955; rpt. New York: Viking Press, 1967), p. xii..

36. Ibid., p. xxii.

37. S. Radhakrishnan, *Eastern Religions and Western Thought* (1939; rpt. London: Oxford Univ. Press, 1940), p. 249.

38. William S. Kennedy, *Reminiscences of Walt Whitman*. quoted by Rao Raypati, p.12.

39. Dorothy F. Mercer, "*Leaves of Grass* and the *Bhagavad Gitā*: A comparative study," Diss. Univ. of Carlifornia 1933, p.l.

40. Ibid., p. 18.

41. Quoted by V.K. Chari, *Whitman in the Light of Vedantic Mysticism:' An Interpretation* (Lincoln: Univ. of Nebraska Press, 1964), p.64.

42. See O.K. Nambiar, *Maha Yogi Walt Whitman: New Light on Yoga* (Bangalore: Jeevan Publications, 1978).

43. Whittier, *The Letters of John Greenleaf Whittier*, ed. John B. Pickard (London: Relknap Press of Harvard Univ. Press, 1975), II, p. 203.

44. Arthur Christy, "Orientalism in New England: Whittier," *American Literature*, I (1929-1930), P. 372.

45. J.G. Whittier, *The Works of John Greenleaf Whittier* (1848; rpt. Boston and New York: Houghton, Mifflin and Co., 1891), II, p. 340.

III

EMERSON AND THE IDEAL OF VEDANTIC MYSTICISM

Numerous books, dissertations and articles have been written on the influence of India on Emerson's thought and writings. This undoubtedly makes the task of a person, who wants to do another dissertation on the same topic, enormously difficult. Other critics have focused attention on aspects like romantic idealism, philosophic utopianism, mystical aspirations and metaphysical quest of Emerson, which taken together, do not make him a spiritual leader of the time. In this dissertation, I want to study these various aspects running through Emerson's thought together as constituting a coherent and unified vision of the universe, a vision embodied in the Indian scriptures which Emerson read. For me, Emerson was the leader of a movement of thought determined by idealism and mysticism. He rejected all dogmas including the dogma of Christianity and stubbornly refused to accept any other external voice except the voice of God arising from within the depth of his heart. Emerson was deeply concerned with such problems as the nature of the universe, the nature of the ultimate reality and the place of man in the universe and man's moral duty etc. We can understand him properly if we try to comprehend the structure of his consciousness, how that consciousness affected his contemporaries and what are its permanent contributions to world thought. Another aspect of Emerson, i.e. his relevance to the contemporary world, has also not been dealt with by anyone. A critic like Stephen E. Whicher says that Emerson's idealism has lost much of its relevance for the modern world. He feels that, "The road he opened to his contemporaries, however, is largely closed to us. Modern thought, as reoriented since Darwin, makes possible and necessary a union of 'Mind' and 'Nature' on a naturalistic basis to which such native Idealism no longer seems relevant. Though we can, and must, share his vision, by a willing suspension of disbelief, if we are to read him at all, relatively few readers now find him a source of faith. Theological seminaries ignore him."[1]

It is difficult to agree with the above view which is based on an incorrect assessment of Emerson's relevance to the modern world. I am inclined to think quite differently. What I propose to do here is to suggest how Emerson has continued to inspire successive generations by his delineation of perennial human problems, problems involving man's place in the Universe. For modern Americans, Emerson has become a source of inspiration. For many mystically-disposed young seekers of truth, Emerson has become a symbol and a fountainhead of new inspiration. "The road he opened to his contemporaries," instead of closing on us, is opening up new vistas of spiritual experience. The naturalistic thought of Darwin is replaced by a new understanding about the universe, and man's role in it. Modern science, especially those branches of physics called high energy physics, sub-atomic or particle physics, is beginning to accept the idealistic and mystical worldview propounded by Emerson and the tradition of the *Upaniṣads* which influenced Emerson. Fritjot Capra in his *The Tao of Physics* explores the parallels between modern physics and Eastern mysticism of which Emerson was a votary.[2] Modern physics, especially in its two branches such as quantum theory and the theory of relativity, has produced startling findings which take physics away from the realm of technology to the realm of philosophy and culture. Its consequence had led to a revision of man's worldview. Physicists like Julius Robert Oppenheimer, Niels Bohr, Werner Heisenberg and Erwin Schrodinger have shown how at the highest stage modern physics and the mystical worldview held by many idealistic traditions come closer to each other. In modern physics the concept of matter of material substance has undergone a complete change. The concepts of space, time, cause and effect have also undergone a radical change. These Concepts are now very much akin to the concepts of Vedānta, Buddhism and Tao. In Capra's words: "... the two foundations of twentieth-century physics-quantum theory and relativity theory-both force us to see the world very much in the way a Hindu, Buddhist or Taoist sees it ...."[3] He goes on to say: ".... modern physics leads us to a view of the world which is very similar to the views held by mystics of all ages and traditions."[4] Hence to say that Emerson's idealism was naive and is no longer relevant is to ignore the present trend of philosophy and science. Whicher considers Emerson's philosophy so remote from modern consciousness that he feels that one needs a "Willing suspension of disbelief" in order to understand him. This seems to be far from truth. His view that "Theological seminaries" ignore him is, however, correct. Emerson was opposed to old Christianity which was based on dogmas and made himself at home with Christian mystics (Meistor Eckhart, Jacob Boehme and Swedenborg) who were looked down upon by the Orthodox Christians as heretics. Therefore, it is natural that modern theological seminaries would ignore him.

Emerson's philosophy was a curious mixture of the idealistic and mystical traditions not only of India but also of many other countries. He was not a realist as we understand the term and his life and teaching were an open indictment of American materialism. This aspect has appealed to the young Americans who are revolting against the worship of Mammon in various forms. The very bedrock of Emerson's philosophy comprises concepts like self-sufficiency of the individual, divinity of human nature, freedom of inquiry, intellectual emancipation, religious freedom, freedom of self-expression and self-reliance and so on. Therefore, it is difficult to agree with Whicher that Emerson has ceased to be relevant.

In the twentieth century, criticism of Emerson has taken various directions.[5] Louis Parrington considers him not as a liberal protestor, but as a conservative social thinker. Yvor Winters goes to the extent of calling him "a fraud and sentimentalist". Yeats and Eliot and a few others have criticised him for lacking a vision of evil. Sherman Paul considers him as a reconciler of knowledge and action. Other critics have seen Emerson as an anticipator of pragmatic philosophy, later propounded by philosophers like Dowey and James. Charles Feidelson regards him as a symbolist very much in line with Ernst Cassirer and Susan Langer. Some of these critics, like Parrington, Sherman Paul and Feidelson, are appreciative of Emerson, while Winters, Yeats and Eliot are negative in their approach. Why Emerson lacks a vision of evil cannot be understood unless one tries to comprehend his concept of the Over-Soul. The influence of Hindu philosophy, especially the Vedantic philosophy, on Emerson accounts for his lack of vision of evil. Emerson who discarded traditional Christianity also discarded the concept of evil inherent in Christianity. F.I. Carpenter (*Emerson and Asia*) and Arthur Christy (*The Orient in American Transcendentalism*) have tried to understand Emerson in the light of Oriental thought, particularly Indian thought, and have, no doubt, opened a new channel of communication in the Emerson scholarship.

The purpose of this chapter is to study Emerson as a philosophical writer interested in idealism and mysticism, an aspect which is central to his thought. His literary aspects are generally taken as expressions of his philosophical concerns. The relationship of his philosophic thought to his literary works is so basic that his literature cannot be studied without his philosophy. In his case, what he says is more important than how he says it. The style of his prose and poetry is influenced by his philosophy and takes on the quality of the sublime. Therefore, a study of his literature inevitably implies a study of his philosophy. The present study seeks to demonstrate the influence of India on his thought.

As it is made clear in the first chapter, the shaping force behind Emerson's thinking was the thought of the idealist thinkers like Kant, Goethe, Coleridge, the Christian mystics and the idealism of the *Upaniṣads*. Idealism is fundamental to Emerson's thought. The sophisticated kind of monistic idealism which the *Upaniṣads* had taught is central not only to Emerson but to the Transcendentalists as a whole. Emerson acknowledges, in unequivocal terms, his love for the Indian religion: "The Indian teaching, through its clouds of legends, has yet a simple and grand religion, like a queenly countenance seen through a rich veil. It teaches to speak the truth, love others as yourself, and to despise trifles. The East is grand, and makes Europe a land of trifles."[6]

Transcendentalism is an idealistic philosophy and it is only as an idealist that Emerson comes very close to the Upaniṣadic philosophy. Idealism implies that the phenomenal world is not the ultimate reality. It has no *Paramarthik Sattā*; in other words the basic assumption of idealism is that the ideas are real and the objective world is unreal. Moreover, idealism emphasizes that mind is prior to matter and not the product of matter. Emerson fully subscribes to the view: "Mind is the only reality, of which men and all other natures are better or worse reflectors."[7] In *Nature*, Emerson writes in a similar vien and admits that true reality lies behind the temporal phenomenon. He mentions approvingly Vyasa and Berkeley who were idealist thinkers: The first and last lesson of religion is, 'the things that are seen, are temporal; the things that are unseen, are eternal.' It puts an affront upon nature. It does that for the unschooled, which philosophy does for Berkeley and Viasa."[8] In the Idealistic philosophy, ultimate truth is an essence, a pure consciousness, not matter. Behind, and within the phenomena there is a spiritual absolute of which phenomena are manifestations. The multitude of things and events which we encounter around us are mnifestations of one ultimate reality; this reality is called

Brahman in Hinduism and the ultimate principle, the Over-Soul, the World-Soul or the ground of Being by other idealists. This "ultimate principle" is undefinable and ungrasable in nature, and is one. In Transcendental-idealistic philosophy dualism is not tenable, as one cannot accept philosophically two independent absolutes. In the Upaniṣadic idealism *Brahman* is the only principle that is the inner essence of all things. It is infinite in nature and beyond all concepts. Everything aroses out of that one single principle. The *Upaniṣads* poetically describe it such:

yathorṇa-nābhiḥ sṛjate gṛhṇate ca, yathā
pṛthivyam oṣadhayas sambhavanti,
yathā sataḥ puruṣāt keśalomāni tathākṣarāt
sambhavatīha viśvam.

[As a spider sends forth and draws in (its thread), as herbs grow on the earth, as the hair (grows) on the head and the body of a living person, so from the Imperishable arises here the universe.][9]

tad etat satyam:
yathā sudīptāt pāvakād visphuliṅgāḥ
sahasraśaḥ prabhavante sarūpāḥ
tathākṣarād vividhāḥ, saumya, bhāvāḥ
prajāvante tatra caivāpi yanti.

[This is the truth. As from a blazing fire, sparks of like form issue forth by the thousands, even so, O beloved, many kinds of being issue forth from the immutable and they return thither too.][10]

Emerson gives voice to these ideas when he writes: "Idealism sees the world in God. It beholds the whole circle of persons and things, of actions and events, of country and religion, not as painfully accumulated, atom after atom, act after act, in an aged creeping past, but as one vast picture which God points on the instant eternity for the contemplation of the soul."[11] Christianity does not believe that God creates the universe out of Himself, that is, God is the material cause of the Universe. The *Upaniṣads* propound that though Brahman creates the universe out of Himself, He is not exhausted by it. The "Invocation" to *Īśa Upaniṣad* describes it thus:

> *Pūrṇam adaḥ, pūrṇam idam, pūrṇāt pūrṇam udacyate*
> *Pūrṇasya pūrṇam ādāya pūrṇam evāvaśiṣyate*
>
> [That is full; this is full. The full comes out of the full. Taking the full from the full the full itself remains.][12]

Materialists, empiricists, behaviourists and classical physicists believe in materialism which considers matter as the ultimate reality. The worldview of materialistic philosophy is based on the engineering model, which means that reality is conceived as a corporeal mass. For the materialists, there is no "ultimate ground of being" or "absolute principle" which is the cause of all causes. Emerson had antipathy to such a philosophy. He believed that a materialist could become an idealist, but an idealist could never opt for materialism. He says: "The foundations of man are not in matter, but in spirit,"[13] and again, "Spirit is the Creator. Spirit hath life in itself. And man in all ages and countries embodies it in his language as the Father."[14] Emerson's aversion to materialism, with its numerous manifestations such as industrialism, love of power, wealth, success, competition etc., was strengthened by his reading of the *Upaniṣads* and the *Bhagavad Gitā*. In the story of Maitreya in the *Bṛhad-aranyaka Upaniṣad* when the sage Yājnavalkya reached the third stage of his life, he wanted to take *Vānaprastha* in order to live in seclusion in the forest and meditate on Brahman. He wanted to divide his property and other material belongings between his two wives, Kātyayani and Maitreyi. Kātyayani who was disposed towards worldly prosperity gladly accepted her share, whereas Maitreyi who was spiritually disposed, refused to accept her share and prayed to her husband to endow her with the knowledge of the ultimate reality. She said: *Yenāhaṁ nāmṛtā syām, kim ahaṁ tena kuryām*, or "what should I do with that by which I do not become immortal?"[15] Maitreyi's refusal to accept wealth and desire, and her prayer for inner wisdom emphasize the Upaniṣadic stress on the primacy of inward life. Emerson, who read the story, was obviously impressed by the anti-materialistic position taken by Maitreyi. He was also impressed by the *Sthitaprajña Yoga* which constitutes the last eighteen verses of the second chapter of the *Bhagavad Gitā*. In these verses Krishna taught Arjuna as to how one should attain equanimity of mind. Charles Wilkins' translation of the verses which Emerson read runs as follows: "A man is said to be confirmed in wisdom when he forsaketh every desire which entereth into his heart, and of himself is happy, and contented in himself. His mind is undisturbed in adversity, he is happy and contented in prosperity, and he is stronger to anxiety, fear, and anger ... The wisdom of that man is established, who in all things is without affection; and, having received good or evil, neither rejoiceth at the one, nor is cast down by the other. His wisdom is confirmed, when, like the tortoise, he can draw in all his members, and restrain them from their wanted purposes."[16]

In materialistic philosophy, only four elements such as earth, water, fire and air are accepted as basic and eternal; either is rejected because it cannot be perceived. In materialism, what is known by direct sense perception is considered as truth. Whatever cannot be perceived directly by senses is considered non-existent. The materialistic philosophy rejects all *a priori* considerations and emphasizes *a posteriori* considerations. It postulates a mechanical non-organic process opposed to the non-mechanical, organic, and holistic view of the Universe. The transcendentalists, particularly Emerson, discard a philosophy which does not take into consideration the human mind. When man is regarded as a mere product of nature it is impossible for him to cherish any kind of ideal. He will simply be tossed in various directions under the pressure of brute forces. Its important drawback is that it denies intuition as a means for knowing the ultimate truth. Emerson writes in *Nature*: "Idealism saith: matter is a phenomenon, not a substance. Idealism acquaints us with the total disparity between the evidence of our own being and the evidence of the world's being. The one is perfect, the other, incapable of any assurance, the mind is a part of the nature of things; the world is a divine dream, from which we may presently awake to the glories and certainties of day."[17] Such a view is totally opposed to the materialistic emphasis on knowledge gained through sense perception. Emerson saw the difference between idealism and materialism clearly and never brought them close to each other. The opposition between the two has been brought out by him succinctly: "What is popularly called Transcendentalism among us is Idealism; Idealism as it appears in 1842. As thinkers, mankind have ever divided into two sects, Materialists and Idealists; the first class founding on experience, the second on consciousness; the first class beginning to think from the date of the senses, the second class perceive that the senses are not final, and say, The senses give us representations of things, but what are the things themselves, they cannot tell. The materialist insists on facts, on history, on the force of circumstances and the animal wants of man; idealist on the power of Thought and of Will, on inspiration, on miracle, on individual culture. These two modes of thinking are both natural, but the idealist contends that his way of thinking is in higher nature. He concedes all that the other affirms, admits the impressions of sense, admits their coherency, their use and beauty, and then asks the materialist for his grounds of assurance that things are as his senses represent them."[18]

Materialism takes the external world as completely real, whereas idealism takes it as an appearance. In Shankar's *Vedānta*, the phenomenal world is conceived as unreal (*Jagat mithyā*). Dr. Radhakrishnan says: "The real is what is present in all times. [*Traikālikādyabādhvatvam.*] It is that which ever was, is and will be [*Kalātrayasattāvat.*] The real cannot be present today and absent tomorrow. The world of experience is not present at all times and is, therefore, not real."[19] Influenced by this Vedāntic concept, Emerson considers the world as appearance and repudiates the materialistic view that the world is real: "... the materialist takes his departure from the external world, and esteems a man as one product of that. The idealist takes his departure from his consciousness, and reckons the world as appearance. The materialist respects sensible masses, Society, Government, social art and luxury, every establishment, every mass, whether majority of numbers, or extent of space, or amount of objects, every social action. The idealist has another measure, which is metaphysical, namely the *rank* which things themselves take in his consciousness; not at all the size or appearance."[20]

In Buddhism also, we find an idealism which is somewhat similar to Shankar's *Advaita Vedantā*. Emerson knew that Buddhism was idealistic in nature when he wrote: "The oriental mind has always tended to this largeness. Buddhism is an expression of it."[21] *Vijānavāda*, a branch of Buddhist philosophy is Transcendental and idealistic in nature. The Buddhist text *Dhammapada* says: "All that we are is the result of what we have thought:it is founded on our thoughts, it is made up of our thoughts. If a man speaks or acts with an evil thought, pain follows him, as the wheel follows the foot of the ox that draws the wagon."[22]

Emerson was influenced by many idealistic traditions, but the one coming from India played an important part in shaping his vision and thought. The original source of his idealism was Plato, and since Plato was influenced by the idealism of the *Upaniṣads* Emerson's idealism became a blend of the *Upaniṣads;* and Plato's. It was Emerson's firm conviction that Plato's fundamental concepts were moulded by the 'Upaniṣadic' idealism: "The unity of Asia and the detail of Europe; ...Plato came to join ... The excellence of Europe and Asia are in his brain."[23] The Platonic concepts such as the complete independence of soul and body, the idea of good, immortality and the concept of fundamental unity suggest that Plato was influenced by the *Upaniṣads*. Emerson's essay on Plato in *Representative Man* "contains the kernel of Emerson's Orientalism."[24] Emerson did not see Plato as an Oriental philosopher but regarded him as a synthesis of "the infinitude of the Asiatic soul" and "the active and creative genius of Europe." Emerson was also influenced by the Neo-Platonists (on whom the influence of Indian mysticism is very much discernible) and the Cambridge Platonists of the seventeenth century.

Emerson was familiar with both the *Bhagavad Gitā* and the *Upaniṣads*. He read *Katha Upaniṣad* in 1856 and composed the poem "Brahma" after reading it. The same year, he read the *Biblioteca Indica* of E. Roer which contained a selection of passages from the *Upaniṣads*. The impression after reading the book was conveyed to Sarah Swain Forbes on May 6, 1857: "I believe I was to send you the true title of the Hindoo book which I admired so much when I read it last summer, the *Upaniṣads*. So I have set it down at full from my memorandum. It is a little book that you must send to London."[25]

The most important Hindu scripture that profoundly impressed Emerson was *The Bhagavat Geeta* (translated by Charles Wilkins, London, 1785,) which he did not read till 1845. He called it "a trans-national book" and held it in high esteem. Asked by L.F. Dimmick if he had any intention of bringing out an American edition of this Hindoo text, he replied that he did not want to give it to people indiscriminately who were not prepared to receive it; if he did this he would surely make the high worth of the book cheap by enabling it to reach vulgar hands.[26] Emerson was maintaining a list of books which he read every year and in that list the *Bhagavad Gitā* was a recurring title. The book was included in his reading list of the years 1845, 1847, 1854, 1867 and 1868. For Emerson, the source of Indian idealism and mysticism was not so much the *Upaniṣads* as the *Bhagavad Gitā*.

Various philosophical, religious and mystical concepts which are woven into the fabric of Emerson's thought are either parallel to Hindu concepts or are directly derived from Hindu scriptures. Of these, the most important is the concept of Over-Soul which is akin to the Upaniṣadic concept of *Brahman*. Emerson elaborates this concept in his essay, "Over-Soul", and in the poem "Brahma." It is pertinent to discuss the genesis of the term "Over-Soul," since the concept is central to Emerson's thought. F.I. Carpenter suggests that Emerson took the term from the Neo-Platonists: "..his (Emerson's) doctrine of the Over-Soul practically *is* Neo-Platonism. It is the theory of spiritual emanation -- the theory that, from an Absolute source, the living water (or sometimes the metaphor is that of light) streams down into all creatures below, imparting to them the divine vital energy."[27] John Smith Harrison is of the opinion that the *Bhagavad Gitā* was Emerson's prototype and the Over-Soul concept has been translated from the word *adhyātma* of the *Bhagavad Gitā*.[28] In the third verse of the eight Chapter of the *Bhagavad Gitā*, the word *Adhyātma* has been used to mean the Supreme Soul:

akṣaraṁ brahma paramaṁ
svabhāvo 'dhyātmam ucyate
bhūtabhāvodbhavakaro
visargaḥ karmasaṁjñitaḥ.

[The imperishable is Brahman, the Supreme. Its dwelling in the individual body is called Adhyatma. The offering which causes the origin of beings is called karma.][29]

Although Carpenter thinks that Emerson's concept of the "Over-Soul" is not derived from his reading of the *Bhagavad Gitā*, the parallel between Emerson's concept and the concept underlying the *Gitā* is enough to suggest that Emerson's thinking is implicitly Oriental.

The technical objection that Carpenter raises, though no doubt valid, cannot be taken as the basis for his opinion. Although Emerson had not read the *Bhagavad Gitā* before the publication of "Over-Soul" in 1841, it cannot be said that he had no idea about the concept before writing the essay. As Cabot suggests, some persons in Concord might have extracted a few important verses from the *Bhagavad Gitā* and shown them to Emerson.[30] It is very likely that Wilkins' translation of the *Gitā*, published in 1785, was available in Boston during the early decades of the nineteenth century. Besides, Jones who highly extolled the teaching of *Gitā* was not unfamiliar to Emerson. His writings might be a possible source of Emerson's knowledge about the concept of *Ādhyatma*. Even though Emerson had not read the *Bhagavad Gitā* before writing "Over-Soul" he had read other books on India, such as William Enfield's *The History of Philosophy, from the Earliest Times to the Beginning of the Present Century* (contains a chapter entitled, "Of the Philosophy of the Indians"); Joseph Priestley's *A Comparison of the Institutions of Moses with those of the Hindoos* (contains a section called "Of the Vedas and other Sacred Books of the Hindoos" and some other sections on Hindoo religion.)[31] It is most likely that Emerson in conceiving of the idea of "Over-Soul" was influenced by Neo-Platonism, Christian mysticism, the *Upaniṣads* and the *Bhagavad Gitā*. The essay, "Over Soul", has striking similarities with the Hindu concept of Brahman.

The notion of *Brahman* as an absolute cosmic principle was first hinted at in the *Ṛig Veda*[32] and was subsequently developed by the Rishis of the *Upaniṣads* and consolidated as a metaphysical concept by the Vedāntic philosophers such as Sankara, Vidyaramya and many others. The development of Indian speculative thought was from polytheism (consisting of 33 million gods) through monotheism to the abstract cosmic principle called *Brahman*. Brahman is the ultimate cause of the universe. Soul and Nature are the manifestations of Brahman. In the *Upaniṣads*, there is a more detailed and clear definition of *Brahman*. It is the power, the primal and eternal energy that lies behind all natural phenomena. It is the life force that pervades the whole universe and everything is illuminated by it.

Brahman has been compared with an inverted tree whose roots are above, and the branches below. That means it is the cause or the genesis of a great cosmic tree whose branches are all the world that we see including ourselves. The simile has been described in *Kaṭha Upaniṣhad* thus:

ūrdhva-mūlo'vāk-śākha eṣo'śvatthas sanātanaḥ,
tad eva śukraṁ tad brahma, tad evāmṛtam ucyate.
tasmin lokāh śritāḥ sarve tad u nātyeti kaś cana:etad vai tat.

[With the root above and the branches below (stands) this ancient fig tree. That (indeed) is the pure; that is Brahman. That, indeed, is called immortal. In it all the worlds rest and no one ever goes beyond it. This verily, is that.][33]

Brahman cannot be defined or known by the mind: the mind being finite cannot measure the infinite which is immeasurable. Human mind can only say what is not Brahman but cannot say what it *is*. In the *Upaniṣads*, Brahman has been described as *neti neti*, not this, not this. The four *mahāvākyaṣ* or the four great vedic statements such as: *aham Brahmasmi* [I am Brahman], *tattvamasi* [Thou art that], *ayamātmā Brahma* [the self is Brahma], *prajñanām Brahma* [Brahma is consciousness], point to the essential oneness of the universal soul, as also, the individual soul. The essence of the whole universe is the invisible Brahman. As the essence of the huge banyan tree is its very small and the invisible seed, the identity of the universal soul and the individual soul is a concept that was intuitively felt long ago by the Indian seekers of truth. In Radhakrishnan's words: "The identity between the subject and object was realised in India before Plato was born."[34] The reason why human beings generally fail to realize this identity is the overpowering domination of *māyā, avidyā* and *ajnāna*.

It is interesting to observe the similarities between Emerson's concept of "Over-Soul" and the Hindu concept of Brahman. The concept of Over-Soul is Emerson's most fundamental concept, other concepts being corollaries or variations of this single concept. As an Unitarian priest Emerson had graduated from believing in the Christian trinity to monotheistic God. The God of the Unitarians, though one and the only God, was still a father figure and a personal God. Unitarianism had a profound liberalizing effect on the minds of the Transcendentalists. It paved the way for Emerson to move from the Unitarian personal God to impersonal Over-Soul which is not a person but is an abstract principle. According to Christy: "... in the doctrine of the Over-Soul the theological pendulum had swung as far towards the Oriental pole as it was possible in New England."[35] Emerson conceived of Over-Soul in the light of the Hindu concept of the Brahman which is an impersonal, eternal, unifying principle. Emerson thus describes the unifying and holistic nature of Over-Soul which is very close to the concept of the Brahman: "...*within man is the soul of the whole; the wise silence; the universal beauty, to which every part and particle is equally related; the eternal ONE*. And this deep power in which we exist, and whose beatitude is all accessible to us, is not only *self-sufficing* and perfect in every hour, but the act of seeing and the thing seen, the seer and the spectacle, *the subject and the object, are one*."[36] (Italics mine.) The "soul of the whole" which is the universal soul or Brahman is also present in man as individual soul. The transcendental spiritual power of the universe, the Over-soul or Brahman when manifested in the individual in an immanent form is called *ātman*. When Emerson says "within man is the soul of the whole," he perhaps means that each individual has in him the Over-Soul or *Parmātman*.

By describing Over-Soul as "the wise silence," Emerson comes very close to the nature of Brahman described in Indian scriptures. The knowledge of Brahman, according to the Indian definition, is possible only through a supracognitive, intuitive power which is above and beyond sense perception. One who has attained the knowledge of the Brahman cannot verbalise it, and therefore the experience remains incommunicable. The experiencer in that state has no separate identity of his own. In that stage knowledge, the knower, and the known become one. This state is described as *turiya* state in the *Upaniṣads*. Therefore, Brahman is rightly regarded as silence. The *Taittirīya Upaniṣad* describes the indeterminable character of the Brahman: *Yato vāco nivartante, aprāpya manasāsaha...* Brahman is that whence words return along with the mind, turn back frustrated.[37] In the *Kena Upaniṣad* there is a similar description:

> *na tatra cakṣur gacchati na vāg gacchati no manaḥ*
> *na vidmo na vijānīmo yathaitad anuśiṣyāt.*

> [There the eye goes not, speech goes not, nor the mind; we know not, we understand not how one can teach this.][38]

The transcendental nature of Brahman is silence. Therefore, it cannot be expressed through words. Sri Aurobindo in his *The Life Divine* describes the nature of ultimate reality as "the transcendent silence."[39] In Buddhism also the ultimate reality is described through silence. Zen Buddhism has its origin in the silence of Buddha. Emerson, who had considerable understanding of Buddhism, knew very well that the nature of ultimate truth is silence which cannot be verbalized. "In Self-Reliance," he gives expression to such a view. For Emerson, as for Zen, intuition, not intellect, is the means by which the highest spiritual realization is possible, and this realization defies communication through words. He remarks: "And now at last the highest truth on this subject (self-reliance) remains unsaid; probably cannot be said; for all that we say is the far-off remembering of the intuition .... The soul raised over passion beholds identity and eternal causation, perceives the self-existence of Truth and Right, and calms itself with knowing that all things go well."[40] The Over-Soul is silence or, as Emerson says, "wise silence." It is the silence of the highest experience. In another passage Emerson reiterates a similar view: "Man is timid and apologetic; he is no longer upright; he dares not say, 'I think,' 'I am,' but quotes some saint or sage. He is ashamed before the blade of grass or the blowing rose. These roses under my window make no reference to former roses or to better ones; they are for what they are: they exist with God today. There is no time to them. There is simply the rose; it is perfect in every moment of its existence.... But man postpones or remembers; he does not live in the present ...We shall not always set so great a price on a few texts, on a few lives."[41]

An obvious corollary of the doctrine of silence is the typical *Upaniṣadic* method of describing *Brahman* in negative terms. The Absolute has been described in the *Upaniṣads* as characterless and attributeless. In the *Kaṭha Upaniṣad*, Brahman is described as, "Without sound, without touch and without form, undecaying, is likewise, without taste, eternal, without smell, without beginning, without end, beyond the great, abiding, by discerning that, one is freed from the face of death."[42]

In *Muṇḍaka Upaniṣad*, Brahman is described as" ... ungraspable, without family, without caste, without sight or hearing, without hands or feet, eternal, all-pervading, omnipresent, exceedingly subtle, that is the Undecaying which the wise perceive as the source of beings."[43] All these suggest, in negative terms, what Brahman is not. As it is difficult to describe

Brahman in positive terms, the only option left for the speculative seer's was to describe it negatively. This famous negative method of the Hindus is known as the *neti neti*, a concept which is often described in the *Bṛhad-āraṇyaka Upaniṣad'*: *"Sa eṣa neti nety ātmā; agṛhyaḥ, na hi gṛahyate..."* "That self is (to be described as) not this, not this. He is incomprehensible for he cannot be comprehended. He is indestructible for He cannot be destroyed. He is unattached for He does not attach himself. He is unfettered. He does not suffer, He is not injured. Indeed, by what would one know the knower? Thus you have the instruction given to you. O *Maitreyī*. Such, verily, is life eternal."[44] When the Brahman is conceived as exclusively a suprapersonal being it cannot have any name whatsoever. The idols (in the Baconian sense) which act as masks and parade as the Brahman are to be discarded in the Upaniṣadic manner, not this, not this, so that reality can be reached directly. Interestingly, as Christy has shown, Emerson was familiar with this method. In an essay, "Demonology," Emerson shows his awareness of the *neti neti* -- a method of the Hindoos. He writes: "My dreams are not me; they are not Nature, or the Not-me: they are both. They have a double consciousness, at once sub-and ob-jective. We call the phantoms that rise, the creation of our fancy, but they act like mutineers, and fire on their commander;[45] Emerson was familiar with the negative method of the *Upaniṣads*.

Emerson describes Over-Soul as the "universal beauty." Universality is the attribute of both Over-Soul and Brahman. Brahman is also described as the embodiment of beauty, because beauty is an aesthetic characteristic of Brahman. So Brahman is Satyam, Sivam and Sundaram or Truth, Good and Beauty. The Over-

Soul is purely holistic and organic in nature. Nothing in the universe exists separately. Each one is related to the other and the Over-Soul passes like a thread (the image of Upaniṣadic *sutrātman* comes to one's mind) through everything that is there in the cosmos. There are numerous verses in *Upaniṣads* which show the inter-relatedness in everything. The idea of organicism and holism is central to Vedanta philosophy. The concept of organicism and holism is related to Emerson's view on the unity of the universe. Emerson's doctrine of polarity and law also emphasizes the unity of the universe. As the following quotation from his "Nature" indicates, Emerson considered everything in the universe as bipolar in nature, that is all objects have negative and positive aspects, and on this ground there is a unity among things: "Each creature is only a modification of the other; the likeness in them is more than the difference, and their radical law is one and the same. A rule of one art, or a law of one organization, holds true throughout nature. So intimate is this Unity that it is easily seen, it lies under the undermost garment of Nature, and betrays its source in Universal Spirit."[46]

This aspect of Emerson's thought has an immediate parallel in the Vedāntic worldview. In fact, the awareness of unity and mutual inter - relation of all things is an important aspect of Eastern mysticism. In Hinduism, Buddhism and Tao there is the doctrine that emphasizes the basic oneness of the cosmos as the manifestation of one underlying and dominating principle variously called *Brahma*, *Dharmakāya*, Tao and *Tathata* (suchness). In our everyday life we divide the world into separate objects and events. But this view of the world is no doubt an illusory one. Because of the predominance of

māyā or *avidyā* on our intellect we fail to see the inherent unity in the universe. Emerson is opposed to such a worldview. He says: "We see the world piece by piece, as the sun, the moon, the animal, the tree; but the whole, of which these are the shining parts, is the soul."[47] All the objects of the world, Emerson thinks, are part of the whole, and the whole is the unifying principle. In *Muṇḍaka Upaniṣad* a similar view is expressed where Brahman is regarded as the unifying thread: "He in whom the sky, the earth and the interspace are woven as also the mind alongwith all the vital breaths, know him alone as the one self. Dismiss other utterances. This is the bridge to immortality."[48] The verb 'weaving' is very significant here. *Tantra*, another important branch of the esoteric Indian system, also propounds such a view. The word "Tantra" itself is etymologically derived from the Sanskrit root *tan* which means "to weave". This means that the whole universe is interwoven with one principle of interdependence of all constituent parts. The aim of a seeker of truth is to finally arrive at a stage where he can intuit the fundamental unity of the universe. According to the Hindu tradition of Yoga and Vedanta, *Samādhi* is the highest state (of the highest of a series of meditative practices such as *Yama*, abstention; *niyama*, observance; *āsana*, posture; *prāṇāyāma*, regulation of breath; *pratyāhāra*, withdrawal of the senses; *dhyāna*, fixed attention; *dhāranā*, contemplation; and *samādhi* concentration) of spiritual progress where one attains a non-dual and beatific vision of oneness and unity. In Emerson's words, "the seer and the spectacle, the subject and object are one." The word *Samādhi* literally means total mental equilibrium. An essential offshoot of Emerson's concept of unity is the unity of all religions in their fundamentals. The concept of the Over-Soul also helps to unify all higher religions of the world. Universal brotherhood was a subject very dear to Emerson. The essential unity between the apparantly discoudant aspects of the universe helped Emerson to look forward to the brotherhood of human beings in the whole world.

Emerson describes the Over-Soul as "self sufficing and perfect," the two qualities which are characteristic sttributes of the Brahman. The Brahman is described as *Purna* (perfect or complete,) *Svaprakāshvān* (self-manifesting, self-sufficient, does not depend on anything external to him) and *Svarāt* (one who is His won master and shines in His own glories.) Emerson's Over-Soul is an impersonal God. According to him, "In all conversation between two persons tacit reference is made, as to a third party, to a common nature. That third party or common nature is not social; it is impersonal; is God."[49] Thought Christy is of the opinion[50] that Emerson never gave a direct answer to the question whether God is personal or impersonal, there are many instances where Emerson unequivocally says that he believes in an impersonal God. When asked, Is God a person? He answered, No.[51] On another occasion Emerson says that God is impersonal. "I deny personality to God because it is too little, not too much."[52] After giving the "Divinity School Address" he was repeatedly asked by theological studends about the true nature of God, Wheter he was personal or impersonal. His answer was: "What shall I answer to these friendly youths who ask me an account of Theism, and think the views I have expressed on the impersonality of God desolating and ghastly? I say, that I cannot find, when I explore my own consciousness, any truth in saying that *God is a person, but the reverse. I feel that there is some profanation in saying. He is personal.* To represent him as an individual is to shut Him out of my consciousness. He is then but a great man such as the crowd worships. Yet, yet, *Cor purgat oratio*."[53] (Italics mine.)

Though Christy thinks that Emerson was not definite in his answer[54] my italics suggest that Emerson's answer gravitated clearly towards the concept of an impersonal God.

Quite early in his career, Emerson moved away from the Judeo-Christian theology and came closer to Hinduism and its impersonal God. There are many instances where he has expressed his dislike of personal anthropomorphic God where He is seen as Lord, Father, Judge and King. His opposition to Christianity is expressed in very clear terms in his "Divinity School Address": "Historical Christianity has fallen into the error that corrupts all attempts to communicate religion. As it appears to us, and as it has appeared for ages, it is not the doctrine of the soul, but an exaggeration of the personal, the positive, the ritual. It has dwelt, it dwells, with noxious exaggeration about the *person* of Jesus. The soul knows no person."[55] Emerson's rejection of a personal anthropomorphic Christian God in favour of an attributeless absolute Brahman or Over-Soul demonstrates his spiritual affinity with Hinduism.

Emerson rejected authority in spiritual matters. His antipathy to Christianity was caused mostly due to the authoritarian and dogmatic aspects of Christianity. His conscience revolted when he was preaching as an Unitarian minister during the time his spiritual conviction was fast moving away from the centre of Christianity. He was not prepared to preach one thing and believe in another. On September 9, 1832, when he was 29, he decided to resign from ministership. His boldness was in consonance with his spirit of revolt against Christianity. In "Over-Soul" he lashes against authority: "The faith that stands on authority is not faith. The reliance on authority measures the decline of religion, the withdrawal of the soul. The position men have given to Jesus, now for many centuries of history, is a position of authority. It characterizes themselves. It cannot alter the eternal facts."[56] He disliked miracles which are considered the bedrock of Christianity and gave his own unorthodox interpretation of miracles.[57] He also disliked the ritualistic practices of Christianity. Swami Parmananda, in his book *Emerson and Vedanta*, writes: "A gentleman once said to Emerson that he had studied all the different philosophies and religions of the world and he was now convinced that Christianity was the only one; to which Emerson replied: That only shows, my friend, how narrowly you have read them."[58] Because of his unorthodox views the clergymen of his time looked down upon him. A Unitarian clergyman, Andrew Norton, dismissed Emerson's mystical teaching and branded it as the "latest form of infidelity." Abner Kneeland, an orthodox believer in Boston, went to the extent of engaging people "to abhor and abominate R.W. Emerson as a sort of mad dog."[59] Emerson, in return, severely criticised the Christian priests for their doctrines like orginal sin, predestination etc. He said that the priests were "diseased with the theological problems of original sin, origin of evil, predestination and the like."[60] His attack on the concept of original sin and his belief in the essential goodness of man are, no doubt, based upon the tenets of Vedantic philosophy. His rejection of authority was followed by his emphasis on the importance of listening to one's own voice from within, which is the voice of God. Emerson says that "by yielding to the spirit of prophecy which is innate in everyman, we can know what it saith."[61] Hinduism and Buddhism have always stressed this aspect. "Look within and thou art the Buddha," so goes the famous saying. "Be a lamp unto thyself" or *ātmadeepobhava*, is also another. Emerson says: "the Bible will not be ended until creation is."[62] He felt that an earnest seeker of truth should listen to one's own voice from within and make one's own Bible: "He must greatly listen to himself, withdrawing himself from all the accents of other men's devotion. Even their prayers are hurtful to him, until he made his own. Our religion vulgarly stands on numbers of believers."[63] "When the intervals of darkness come, as come they must-- when the sun is hid and the stars withdraw their shining -- we repair to the lamps which were kindled by their ray, to guide our steps to the East again, where the dawn is."[64]

Time and space are two fundamental concepts for understanding the world around us. Emerson's views on time and space are similar to those held by *Vedānta*, Buddhism and the mysticism of the East in general. According to *Vedānta*, time and space and causation are constructs of the mind and are therefore, ultimately unreal. Like all other intellectual concepts these are illusory and relative. We use these categories in order to describe aspects of reality and believe in their ultimate truth and validity. Just as there is a difference between the map of a country and the country itself, there is a difference between the ultimate reality and its map which is a mental construct. Time and space are part of the map; they indicate reality and do not actually constitute its territory. Therefore, to consider them as ultimately true is wrong. *Vedānta* suggests that time and space have no real existence of their own. They are only names and forms of thought. "Time, space and causation are like the glass through which the Absolute is seen... In the Absolute there is neither time, space or causation."[65] When one attains a state of *Samādhi* (stillness) the notion of time and space vanishes; only an eternal 'now' remains. The seeker bathes in the glow of eternity. In Emerson's words: "With each divine impulse the mind rends the thin rinds of the visible and finite, and comes out into eternity, and inspires and expires its air."[66] His views of time and space, thus, fully agree with the Hindu and Buddhist concepts of time and space. He writes: "The soul circumscribes all things. As I have said, it contradicts all experience. In like manner it abolishes time and space."[67] He continues: "...the soul's scale is one, the scale of the senses and the understanding is another. *Before the revelations of the soul, Time, Space and Nature shrink away*."[68] (Italics mine.) As stated earlier Emerson holds the view, like the Indian mystics, that time and space vanish when one attains spiritual enlightenment. The Buddhist philosophers also hold a similar view. *Mādhyamika kārika vṛtti* have the following lines which epitomize the Buddhist view of time and space: "... Space, Time and Nirvāna were mere forms of thought or words of common usage...If time too is conceived to be variable, it would be non - existent at times, or be impermanent like the seed. And for this, it would have to be dependent on conditions on the occurrence of which it would happen and without which it would not."[69] It is interesting to point out here that the views held by the Indian mystics and Emerson concerning time and space are corroborated by modern physics. In classical physics, space was regarded as absolute, three-dimensional reality. It was considered independent of the objects of the world. Time, like space, was also regarded as something absolute. But in Einstein's theory of relativity time and space are considered relative, and time constitutes the fourth dimension.

The moment of spiritual enlightenment, which is linked with the concepts of time and space, has been described by Emerson exactly in the manner of the Hindu mystics. According to him, "A certain tendency to insanity has always attended the opening of the religious sense in men, as if they had been 'blasted with excess of light'. The trances of Socrates, and 'Union' of Plotinus, the vision of Porphyry, the conversion of Paul, the aurora of Behmen, the convulsions of George Fox and his Quakers, the illumination of Swedenborg, are of this kind .... that shudder of awe and delight with which the individual soul always mingles with the universal soul."[70] The highest spiritual experience in the awakening of *Kundalini in Samādhi, nirvāna* and *Satori* has always been described by the Indian mystics in the manner of Emerson. "A certain tendency to insanity" that arises in individuals at the time of spiritual enlightenment approximates that state of mental quivering at the moment of the awakening of *Kundalini*. The Vaishnava devotee at the peak of his devotion has always shown emotional intensity which verges on madness. In *Bhagavat Purāna* there is a verse where a spiritually enlightened person is described as mad:

evmvratah swaprryānamakirtyā
jātāmurāgo dṛtachitta uchchiah
hasatyathou roditi rauti gaya
tunmadabannṛtyati lokabāhyah.

[His heart melts through Love as he habitually chants the Name of his beloved

> Lord in this way, and like one (mad person,) he now bursts into peals of laughter, now weeps, now cries, now sings aloud and now begins to dance in a singular way.][71]

Emerson's poem "Brahma" crystallizes many concepts taken from Indian sources. The poem was published in the first number of *Atlantic Monthly* in November 1857, and subsequently in the volumes of 1867 and 1876. It became a controversial poem from the very beginning because of its anti-Christian attitude and its direct treatment of the Upaniṣadic mysticism. While discussing with his daughter the controversy raised by the poem, Emerson said, perhaps in anger, "Tell them to say Jehovah instead of Brahma."[72] In 1876, when a selection of his poems was about to be published his publishers asked him to change the title of the poem as it had aroused a lot of controversy. But Emerson refused to change the title. The poem was not properly understood by critics because they were not familiar with Hindu thought. Even a great writer like Carlyle described it as "pale moonshine."[73] R.L. Rusk writes: "Brahma provoked the laughter of those who were ignorant of Hindu love -- and they must have comprised most of the readers of *The Atlantic*"[74]. Critics like W.T. Harris, W.S. Kennedy, F.I. Carpenter, Arthur Christy, L. Goren, K.R. Chandrasekharan who have written about this poem are almost unanimous in their view that the poem could not have been written without the influence of the *Kaṭha Upaniṣad* and the *Bhagavad Gitā*. F.I. Carpenter says that this poem expresses the fundamental Hindu concept "more clearly and concisely than any other writing in the English language -- perhaps better than any writing in Hindu literature itself."[75] To W.T. Harris, the poem is a "wonderful summary of the spirit of the Indian mind."[76] The following is the full text of the poem to enable the readers to refer to it when I analyse it in terms of its content of Hindu thought:

BRAHMA

If the red slayer think he slays,
    Or if the slain think he is slain,

They know not well the subtle ways
    I keep, and pass, and turn again.

Far or forgot to me is near;
    Shadow and sunlight are the same;

The vanished gods to me appear;
    And one to me are shame and fame.

They reckon ill who leave me out;
    When me they fly, I am the wings;

I am the doubter and the doubt,
    And I the hymn the Brahmin sings.

The strong gods pine for my abode,
    And pine in vain the sacred Seven;

But thou, meek lover of the good!
    Find me, and turn thy back on heaven.[77]

The title of the poem has created a certain amount of confusion. The title "Brahmā" has been mistaken for Brahma. F.I. Carpenter says that "In *Brahmā*-- the impersonal creative force of the world, is represented as the speaker."[78]

By this Carpenter understands Brahma as *Brahmā*, one of the gods in the Hindu trinity. This mistake has been rightly pointed out by K.R. Chandrasekharan in his article "Emerson's Brahma: An Indian Interpretation."[79] Brahma actually means the universal Soul, the Absolute or "Over-Soul." The poem does not have any reference to Brahmā, the creator but it contains all the attributes and qualities of Brahma, the ultimate reality. Chandrasekharan's observation that the proper title should have been *Brahman* is not necessarily correct, for *Brahmā* and *Brahman* are synonymous.

Emerson got the central idea of the poem from his reading of *Kaṭha Upaniṣad* which was included in the *Bibliotheca Indica* (Calcutta, 1852). The following verse from *Kaṭha Upaniṣad* forms the basis of the first few lines of the poem:

> *hantā cen manvate hantuṁ hates' cen*
> *manyate hatam.*
> *ubhau tau na vijānīto nāyaṁ hanti*
> *na hanyate.*[80]

> [If the slayer thinks I slay, if the slain thinks I am slain, then both of them do not know well, it (the soul) does not slay nor is it slain.][81]

Subsequently, Emerson noted down this idea in his *Journals* in various contexts.[82] This Upaniṣadic theme has also been employed with a slight modification in the *Bhagavad Gitā*: "The Atman is neither born nor does it die. Coming into being and ceasing to be do not take place in it. Unborn, eternal constant and ancient. It is not killed when the body is slain."[83] The phrase "red slayer" is, however, Emerson's own coinage and refers to any slayer whose hands are gory with human blood. The image is a vivid one and conjures up the picture of a killer who is smeared with blood and consequently looks red. The image of the *Kshatriya* warriors who were professional enemy killers may have prompted Emerson to coin the expression "red slayer." K.R. Chandrasekharan, however, gives a different interpretation to the word "red slayer." He compares the "red slayer" with Rudra,[84] the God of destruction, a comparison which is not at all appropriate. Emerson puts these words into the mouth of the Absolute or Over-Soul who is actually an impersonal being. It would be more appropriate to put them into the mouth of the speaker of the *Bhagavad Gitā*, Lord Krishna, who is regarded as an immanent form of the Absolute (*Kṛshnastū Bhagabān Svayam*). Krishna himself is God or the Absolute. The poem is a justification of the subtle ways of *Brahman* or Over-Soul to man and expresses a higher truth which is not likely to be understood by an ordinary human being. Arjuna was puzzled because for him the slain and the slayer were different. This puzzlement arose out of his egoism. A man, dominated by his ego, would call himself a doer, but in the ultimate analysis there is no difference between the man who acts, and the man who is acted upon. Thus the slayer and the slain, the doubter and the doubt, are one.

In the second stanza the influence of another Upanisadic verse is clearly discernible. In the *Upaniṣads* there are many paradoxical descriptions of the *Brahman*. The *Upaniṣads* say the Brahman moves and does not move; He is far and near. The following verse embodies the paradoxical nature of the Brahman: "It moves and It moves not; It is far and it is near; It is within all this and It is also outside all this."[85] In the Supreme Being the Brahman, the ordinary mental constructs such as distance and nearness which imply space; past and present implying time; light and darkness, shame and fame, victory and defeat do not exist. All the oppositions and conflicts vanish in Him. The earthly differences which are relative in nature are embraced by the unity of the Brahman. The concept of good and bad is based on human reasoning, and suggests contrasting principles. Pleasure and pain, success and failure, life and death are based on dichotomies which are, in the ultimate analysis, illusory motions. A Zen poem says: "The conflict between right and wrong is the sickness of the mind." The fundamental idea of Buddhism is to transcend these earthly opposites.

In the *Bhagavad Gitā*, Srikrishna talks repeatedly about going beyond the world of opposites.[86] The Brahman or Over-Soul has such a unity where all distinctions disappear. Emerson, in his poem, "Celestial Love," describes this unity thus:

> Where good and ill,
> And joy and moan,
> Melt into one,
> There Past, Present, Future, shoot
> Triple blossoms from one root;
> Substances at base divided,
> In their summits are united.[87]

In another poem "Wood-Notes" also he gives expression to such a concept:

> Alike to him the better, the worse,-
> The glowing angel, the outcast corse.[88]

The third stanza of "Brahma" is clearly influenced by the tenth chapter of the *Bhagavad Gitā* where Lord Krishna gives a long catalogue of things in which he is present as the Supreme Being. The last line of the stanza is particularly similar to the line in the *Bhagavad*

Gitā: Vedānam Sāmavedosmi.... [Of the Vedas I am the Sama; I am Vasava among the Devas; of the senses I am the mind and among living beings I am consciousness.][89] The fourth and the concluding stanza is once again influenced by the *Upaniṣads* and the *Bhagavad Gitā*. The "strong gods" here are perhaps Indra (the king of the gods), Agni, (the god of fire), Yama (the god of death), Varuna (the god of the seas), Kubera (the god of wealth). The "sacred seven" refers to the seven ṛishis such as Kratu, Pulaha, Pulastya, Atri, Angirā, Vasistha and Marichi. These ṛishis preside over *manavantaras*. The last two lines emphasize the Upaniṣadic dismissal of rituals and sacrifices which were a means to attain heaven. One who is bent upon realizing Brahman could not stop at the promises of heaven. Heaven is not a permanent abode of peace. After the exhaustion of one's own *Karmaphala* (the fruits of labour,) one is thrown from heaven. According to *Gitā*: "Having enjoyed the vast world of heaven, they return to the world of mortals on the exhaustion of their merits; thus abiding by the injunctions of the three Vedas, desiring objects of desires they go and come."[90] Emerson puts this idea forcefully in the last line of the poem: "find me, and turn thy back on heaven." A true spiritual seeker always turns his back on the so-called heaven. Both the *Upaniṣads* and the *Bhagavad Gitā* have avowedly declared the uselessness of action as a means to liberation and have emphasized knowledge as the only means for attaining *moksha* (salvation). Emerson subscribes to such a view in the last two lines of the poem. Besides "Brahma," the other poems which are profoundly influenced by Hindu concepts are "Hamatreya," "Wood-Notes," "The Celestial Love," "Sphinx" and "Spirit."

Another important Hindu philosophical concept which became a part of Emerson's thinking is *Māyā*. The concept of *Māyā* is the very basis of *Vedānta* philosophy. In Hindu scriptures the word first occurred in the *Ṛg Veda* where it was used in a limited sense. In *Ṛg Veda*, it connotated super-natural power or wonderful skill.[91] In *Atharva Veda*, "māyā" meant magical power or illusion. In the *Upaniṣads* the concept of *māyā* became the central philosophy and in Sankara's *Advaita* philosophy it got its full conceptual clarity. According to *Advaita Vedānta*'Brahma is the only reality, and therefore the phenomenal world which is diverse cannot be real as there cannot be two ultimate realities. Either the Brahman or the phenomenal world is real, but both cannot be real in a non-dual vision of the universe. For an idealist like Vedāntin, the Brahman is the only reality, and for a materialist the phenomenal world is the only reality. For the *Advaitin*, those who take the world for the real are deluded and are under the spell of *māyā*. As the *Bhagavad Gitā* says:

nā 'sato vidyate bhāvo
nā bhāvo vidyate sataḥ
ubhayor api dṛṣṭo 'ntas tv
anayos tattvadarśibhiḥ.

[The unreal has no existence; the real never ceases to be. The truth about both has been realized by the seers.][92]

Māyā is the cosmic illusion and a deceptive veil that obscures our vision and prevents us from seeing the truth in its true colour. The *Upaniṣads* compares it with a golden veil: *Hiraṇmayena pātṛeṇa satyasyāpihitam mukham.* "The face of truth is covered with the golden disc."[93]

Māyā has two functions. The first is known as *ābaranashakti* and conceals the true nature of the real. The second, called *Vikshep shakti* projects the unreal. It prevents the individual from perceiving the unity of the infinite Brahman, and in that sense it is a negative force. It is the result of *avidyā* or ignorance. With the dawn of true knowledge the veil of *māyā* disappears and the Brahman is intuitively felt.

Throughout Emerson's writings, the concept of *māyā* is used on several occasions. The essay, "Illusion", has a reference to *Yoganidrā*, "the goddess of illusion". *Māyā* is also referred to as the illusory power of Vishnu or, as Emerson says, "successive maias of Vishnu". The earliest influence of the concept of *māyā* on Emerson came probably during his Harvard days when he read "A Hymn to Nārāyena." In 1820, he read Sir William Jones' translation of "Narayena" along with other Hindu poems. The germs of the concept of *māyā* might have taken root in his thinking during the period. The lines from "Nārāyena" which contain the seeds of *māyā* are:

> Primeval MAYA was the Goddess nam'd,
> Who to her fire, with Love divine inflam'd,
>
> X X X X X X
>
> In air, in floods, in caverns,
> woods, and plains;
> Thy will inspirits all,
> thy sov'reign MAYA reigns.[94]

The poem, "Maia," conveys a fine idea of the Hindu theory of illusion. As Christy tells us, Emerson "called his own thoughts the doctrine of illusion, but he recognized their resemblance to Maya, and he admitted that the

Hindus had treated the subject with the greatest catholicity. Whether he was right or not, Emerson accepted the doctrine as fundamental."[95] Emerson's firm conviction was that the phenomenal world had no ultimate reality. Emerson believed that *māyā* is a power by which the Over-Soul or Brahman creates the phenomenal world. He remarks: "God is a reality and his method is illusion."[96] This idea is elaborately described by Emerson in one of his journal entries:

> *Māyā* (Illusion) *of the Hindoos*. Rudra says, O thou, who, always unalterable, createst, conservest, and destroyest this universe, by the aid of Maya, that energy in numerous forms which ... makes believe that it is distinct from thee, and gives to the world an apparent reality.
>
> *Maya* ....
>
> The Veda says: 'The world is born of Maya.' 'Brahma' qui n'a pas de qualities.[97]

Like the concept of *māyā*, the law of *Karma* is another fundamental Hindu doctrine which Emerson believed in. It is also related to the doctrines of rebirth, transmigration of soul and the principle of good and evil. Emerson was considerably influenced by the Law of *karma* and the related concepts. The law of *Karma* was first discussed in the *Satpatha Brāhmana* and later in the *Upaniṣads*. It's fundamental assumption is that no action is ever wasted. In human life virtue is rewarded, and vice punished. It becomes the moral foundation of the universe and can be called the law of moral retribution. *Karma* implies that every action has its reaction. It presupposes that any effect we discover in this life has a cause in our past *karma*. Based on the immutable principle of cause and effect, this Law accounts for the cause of every individual and human event including suffering and joy. According to Hinduism nothing happens through chance or coincidence, whatever happens is determined by *karma* of this life or *karma* of the past life. What we call fate is actually the accumulated *karma* of the past which has become ripe for execution and its effect cannot be stayed. It is bound to happen, its force being like that of a huge avalanche which slides down a hill and cannot be checked. The fruit of right *karma* which must have its effect without our foreknowledge is called fate or destiny. In a sense the Law of *karma* is independent of God.

Karma and rebirth or transmigration are two integrated principles. With this is also associated the idea of immortality. Soul, being immortal, does not die with the death of an individual. It looks forward to another life if it is not finally liberated. The sum total of one's good and bad *karma* remains tied with the *jīvatmā* or individual soul in a very subtle form. It takes another birth according to the person's own *karma*. If his deeds are good (*punya*) he takes a body where there are greater opportunities; if his deeds are bad (*pāap*) he takes a body where there are less opportunities. When a person realizes the *Brahman* he becomes free for ever from the wheel of birth and death or, in other word, he never experiences transmigration.

In this doctrine of the Law of *karma* and rebirth Emerson found a very cogent explanation of the riddle of suffering and joy in human life. Supporting the Law of *karma* he writes in the essay "Compensation": "You cannot do wrong without suffering wrong."[98] And "Every secret is told, every crime is punished, every virtue rewarded, every wrong redressed, in silence and certainty. What we call retribution is the universal necessity by which the whole appears wherever a part appears."[99] In another essay "Worship," he says that every service is rewarded: "He is great, whose eyes are opened to see that the reward of actions cannot be escaped, because he is transformed into his action, and taketh its nature." [100] Buddhism also believes in the doctrine of the Law of *karma*'and rebirth. Emerson who had a fair knowledge of Buddhism quotes approvingly the Buddhist doctrine of karma in the essays "Worship" and "The Transcendentalist." The following passages bear ample testimony to this. "The Buddhists say, 'No seed will die': every seed will grow. Where is the service which can escape its remuneration ?"[101] And "The Buddhist, who thanks no man, who says, 'Do not flatter your benefactors', but who, in his conviction that every good deed can by no possibility escape its reward, will not deceive the benefactor by pretending that he has done more than he should, is a Transcendentalist."[102]

For the Hindus, there is no such thing as fate. What Hindus called *adṛsta* is the result of right *karma* which is both invisible and invincible. Emerson's idea of fate, although mixed up with the Islamic concept of *kismet*, is closer to the Hindu concept:

> It was a poetic attempt to lift this mountain of Fate, to reconcile this despotism of race with liberty, which led the Hindoos to say, 'Fate is nothing but the deeds committed in a prior state of existence'....To say it less sublimity. In the history of the individual is always an account of his condition, and he knows himself to be a party to his present estate.[103]

As a young man, Emerson believed in his own personal immortality, but later he gave up the idea of individual immortality. He writes: "I confess that everything connected with our personality fails. Nature never spares the individual".[104] His rejection of individual immortality does not imply rejection of the immortality of soul. Like the Unitarians and the Hindus, he believed in the continuity of life; he believed that the next life would be saved not by the arbitrary decree of a tyrannical Jehovah, but according to the strict law of *karma* which is a logical conclusion of his law of compensation. The following statements unmistakably establish Emerson's conviction regarding the reality of rebirth. "I believe in this life. I believe it continues."[105] "Travelling the path of life through thousands of births,"[106] was an entry in his *Journals*, a statement which suggests that Emerson believed in the cycle of continuity. He remarks: "that all things subsist, and do not die, but only retire a little for sight and afterwards return again."[107]

Footnotes:

1. Stephen E. Whicher, *Selections from Ralph Waldo' Emerson* (1957; rpt. Boston: Houghton, 1960), Intro.p.XVII.

2. Fritjot Capra, *The Tao of Physics* (1975; rpt.Suffolk Fontana/Collins,1978).

3. Ibid., p. 17.

4. Ibid.

5. Stephen E.Whicher, *Emerson: A Collection of Critical Essays*, ed. M.Konvitz and S.Whicher (N.J.: Prentice-Hall, Inc., 1962), Pref.V-VIII.

6. Emerson, *Journals*, 1845, VII, 129-130

7. Emerson, *Complete Works*, I. p. 333. (The Transcendentalist).

8. Ibid., p. 58. (Nature)

9. *Principal Upaniṣads*, p.673. (Muṇḍaka,I:I.7)

10. Ibid., p. 679-680. (Muṇḍaka, II:I.I)

11. *Complete Works*, I, P.60. (Nature)

12. *Principal Upaniṣads*, p. 566. (Īśa Upaniṣad)

13. *Complete Works*, I,p.70. (Nature)

14. Ibid., p. 27.

15. *Principal Upaniṣads*, p.195-196. (Bṛahad-āraṇyaka, II:4:2-3)

16. "The Bhagavat-Geeta," tr. Charles Wilkins, *American Transcendental Quarterly*, I, 20(Fall, 1973), p. 33.

17. *Complete Works*, I.p. 62 (Nature)

18. Ibid., pp. 329-330. (The Transcendentalist)

19. S. Radhakrishnan, *Indian Philosophy*, (1923; rpt.London:George Allen & Unwin Ltd.,1966), II. p. 562.

20. *Complete Works*, I. p. 332-333. (The Transcendentalist).

21. Ibid., p.337

22. *The Dhammapada*, tr. Irving Babbitt (1936; rpt. New York: New Directions Books, 1965), I:1, p. 3.

23. *Complete Works*, IV, p. 40. (Plato; or, the Philosopher).

24. Carpenter, *Emerson and Asia*, p. 14.

25. Emerson, *Letters*, V. p. 70

26. Ibid., IV. p. 350-351.

27. *Emerson and Asia*, p.75

28. John S. Harrison, *The Teachers of Emerson* (New York:Haskell House, 1966), p. 277-278.

29. *Bhagavad Gita*, p. 452-453. (VIII:3).

30. See Kurt F. Leidecker, "Emerson and East-West Synthesis," *Philosophy East and West*, I, 2 (July,1951), p.44.

31. See K.W.Cameron, "More Notes on Orientalism in Emerson's Harvard," *ESQ*, 22 (I Qrt., 1961), p.81-90.

32. *Ṛg Veda*, x:82.

33. *Principal Upaniṣads*, p.641. (Katha, II:3:1).

34. *Indian Philosophy*, I. p. 169

35. Christy, *The Orient*, Intro. p.21

36. *Complete Works*, II, p. 269. (The Over-Soul)

37. *Principal Upaniṣads*, p. 545. (Taittiriya, II:4:1)

38. Ibid., p. 582. (Kena, II:3)

39. Sri Aurobindo, *The Life Divine* (Calcutta: Arya Publishing House, 1939), I.p.34

40. *Complete Works*, II. pp. 68-69. (Self-Reliance).

41. Ibid., p. 67.

42. *Principal Upaniṣads*, pp. 628-629. (Kaṭha, I:3:15)

43. Ibid., pp. 672-673. (Mundaka, I:I:6)

44. Ibid., pp. 286. (Bṛhad-āraṇyaka, VI:5:15)

45. *Complete Works*, x, pp. 7-8. (Demonology)

46. Ibid., I, pp. 44-45. (Nature)

47. Ibid., II, p. 269. (The Over-Soul)

48. *Principal Upaniṣads*, pp. 683-684. (Muṇḍaka, II:5)

49. *Complete Works*, II, p. 277. (The Over-Soul)

50. Christy, *The Orient*, p. 79.

51. *Journals*, IV, 185.

52. Ibid., p. 416.

53. Ibid., p. 404.

54. *The Orient*, p. 80.

55. *Complete Works*, I, p. 130 (An Address).

56. Ibid., II, p. 295. (The Over-Soul).

57. Paul F. Boller, *American Transcendentalism, 1830-1860:An Intellectual Inquiry* (New York: G.P.Putnam's Sons, 1974), p.5.

58. Swami Paramananda, *Emerson and Vedanta* (Boston:The Vedanta Centre, 1918), p. 9.

59. Robert Clifton Whittemore, *Makers of the American Mind* (New York: William Morrow & Co., 1964).

60. *Complete Works*, II, p. 132. (Spiritual Laws)

61. Ibid., p. 269. (The Over-Soul).

62. *Journals*, IX, 15.

63. *Complete Works*, II.pp. 294-295. (The Over-Soul).

64. Ibid., I, p. 91. (The American Scholar).

65. Swami Vivekananda, *Jnana Yaga* (Calcutta: Advaita Ashram, 1972), p. 109.

66. *Complete Works*, II, p.275. (The Over-Soul)

67. Ibid., p. 272.

68. Ibid., p. 273.

69. T.R.V. Murti, *The Central Philosophy of Buddhism* (1955; rpt. London: George Allen & Unwin, 1960), p. 198.

70. *Complete Works*, II, p.281-282. (The Over-Soul).

71. *The Philosophy of Love: Bhakti-Sutra of Devaraj Narada*, tr.Hanumanprasa Poddar (Rajgangpur: Orissa Cement Ltd., n.d.), p. 31. (Srīmad Bhagavata, XI:II:40)

72. Robert, L. White, "Emerson's 'Brahma," *The Explicator*, XXI (April, 1963), No.8. Item.63.

73. Charles Malloy, "A Study of Emerson's Major Poems" (BRAHMA) *American Transcendental Quarterly*, I (Summer, 1974), p. 62.

74. R.L Rusk, *The Life of Ralph Waldo Emerson* (New York:Charles Scribner's Sons, 1949), p.396.

75. *Emerson and Asia*, p. 111.

76. W.T. Harris, "Emerson's Orientalism," in *Concord Harvest*, ed. K.W. Cameron (Hartford: Transcendental Books, 1970), l.p. 187.

77. *Complete Works*, IX, p. 195 (BRAHMA)

78. *Emerson and Asia*, p. 113.

79. K.T.R.Chandrasekharan, "Emerson's *Brahma*: An Indian Interpretation," *The New England Quarterly*,,XXXIII, 4 (Dec..,1960), pp. 506-512.

80. *Principal Upaniṣads*, p. 616.(Kaṭha, I:2:19).

81. This translation is the original one which Emerson read in *Bibliotheca Indica* (Cal., 1852). see W.S.Kennedy, "Clews to Emerson's Mystic

Verse," *American Transcendental Quarterly* 3 (Winter, 1976), p. 6.

82. *Journals*, VI, 1844, 494; 1845, VII, 127.

83. *Bhagavad Gita*, p.139. (II:20).

84. Chandrasekharan, p. 507.

85. *Principal Upaniṣads*, p. 571. (Īśa, 5)

86. *Bhagavad Gita*, pp. 185-187. (II: 56-57)

87. *Complete Works*, IX, p.115. (The Celestial Love)

88. Ibid., p. 59. (Woodnotes II)

89. *Bhagavad Gita*, p.549. (X:22)

90. Ibid., p. 506. (IX:21).

91. *Indian Philosophy*, I., 103-104. (Ṛg. Veda, VI:47:18).

92. *Bhagavad Gita*, p. 134. (II:16)

93. *Principal Upaniṣads*, p. 577. (Īśa,15)

94. "A Hymn to Nārāyena," p. 581-583.

95. *The Orient*, p. 86

96. *Journals*, VII, 505.

97. Ibid., X, 159.

98. *Complete Works*, II,p. 110. (Compensation).

99. Ibid., p. 102.

100. Ibid., VI.p. 231. (Worship)

101. Ibid.

102. Ibid., l, p. 337. (The Transcendentalist)

103. Ibid., VI, pp. 12-13. (Fate)

104. Ibid., VIII, pp. 342-343. (Immortality)

105. *Journals*, III. 210.

106. Ibid., VII, 94.

107. *Journals*, VI, 494. also IX, 552.

IV
THOREAU AS A YANKEE YOGI

Henry David Thoreau (1817-1862) has been a controversial writer in the history of American literature. His life and writings are so unlike other American writers and thinkers that during the last one century critics have tended to regard him as a transcendental crank and "a speaker and actor of the truth...,"[1] as well. Assessment of his work has always been extreme. Those who have not understood him have condemned him in most scathing terms and those who have understood him have eulogised him in superlative terms. For instance, John Burroughs has called him a wild man akin to the American Indian[2] and Havelock Ellis has compared him with a cynic like Diogenes.[3] There are still others who estimate him as a thorough-going misanthropist and a political anarchist. His unusual life and his multifaceted writings have, no doubt, given scope for these extreme assessments. In fact, for Americans Thoreau was a quirky man given to extremes. His grand philosophic aloofness, his hatred of materialism, society, and citics his lack of ambition, his yogic renunciation and austerity, his love of solitude, his excessive love of nature, resulting and his refusal to cooperate with a government whose policies he did not approve of, were certain extreme traits likely to be misunderstood. Besides, he was a vegetarian, a non-smoker, and a tetotaller. He remained a bachelor throughout his life, walked hundreds of miles, avoided inns, and prefered to sleep by the railroad, never voted and never went to a church, derived spiritual inspiration from the Hindu scriptures like the *Bhagavad Gitā* and the *Laws of Manu* living an extremely frugal and spartan life. Though a Harvard University graduate, he never took up a conventional career and instead earned his living by doing sundry odd jobs such as teaching, pencilmaking, land surveying, writing in magazines, fence building, gardening, whitewashing and farming (beans for example). All these apparently incongruous traits in his character made him a bit of an odd ball. Emerson-Thoreau's neighbour, friend, spiritual guide and mentor-said in Thoreau's funeral sermon (later revised and published as an essay) in the following manner: "At this time, a strong, healthy youth, fresh from college, whilst all his companions were choosing their profession, or eager to begin some lucrative employment, it was inevitable that his thoughts should be exercised on the same question, and it required rare decision to refuse all the accustomed paths and keep his solitary freedom at the cost of disappointing the natural expectations of his family and friends: all the more difficult that he had a perfect probity, was exact in securing his own independence, and in holding every man to the like duty. But Thoreau never faltered. He was a born protestant. He declined to give up his large ambition of knowledge and action for any narrow craft or profession, aiming at a much more comprehensive calling, the art of living well."[4]

Thoreau showed unusual traits very early in his life. During childhood he showed certain potentialities of character which were to bloom later. For example, unlike other children, he showed little enthusiasm for games, parades and playing of bands. Instead he went to the forests and hillsides to pluck berries. After completing his grammer school he joined the Harvard University on the August 30, 1983. During his stay in Harvard he spent most of his leisure hours in the university library. He was a voracious reader and used to borrow a large number of books from the library. The only other thing he liked most was observating nature. Books were his constant companions, and he was seldom seen without a book in hand. It is interesting to note here that during his stay at Harvard, Thoreau did not read a single book pertaining to India, although the Harvard library was rich in such books. As Christy says: "It is a singular fact that not a single Oriental volume appeared on the record of Thoreau's reading as an undergraduate at the Harvard College Library. He probably contracted the enthusiams from Emerson. It was during the residence in his friend's home in the year 1841 that Thoreau's extravagant outpouring of praise for the Eastern books commenced."[5]

His love for nature also developed during that period. He used his leisure roaming the fields of Cambridge, and the banks of the Charles river. He led a quiet life at Harvard except for an event like Dunkin Rebellion. He left Harvard in 1837 with a clean record. After graduating from Harvard, he was required to embark upon a profession by selecting a suitable job. Those were the days of economic depression and it was not very easy to find a job. But luckily Thoreau got a teaching job in the Public Grammar School, his *alma mater*. Teaching suited more to his temperament than other professions . But within a fortnight of joining he got involved in a controversy with the school of authorities on the issue of corporal punishment. By temperament he had an innate hatred for cruelty of any kind and, was therefore averse to flogging the children. He was not prepared to compromise on this issue and resigned.

This incident highlights many significant traits in his nature. It signifies his love for children, his hatred of cruelty, his rebellious spirit, his individualism, and his love of freedom. Cruelty and violence are absolutely foreign to his nature, a character trait which a Brahmin should ideally posses. We are reminded here of an anecdote from the *Vedas'* The story goes that a Vedic *ṛshi* asked his young son to collect a donkeyload of *samidhā* (firewood used for sacrifice). The boy in obedience to his father's orders took the donkey out to the forest and overloaded it with firewood. He continued to beat the donkey even when it was faltering, unable to carry the load. Back home, the donkey told its mother about the cruel treatment meeted to him by the Brahmin's son. To this, the donkey's mother replied that the boy was not born of Brahmin father. Had he been born to a Brahmin he could not have been so cruel, for cruelty is foreign to a Brahmin's nature. Inquires showed that the donkey was right. This anccdote suggests that Thoreau's nature was very close to a true Brahmin's. As no teaching job was available immediately Thoreau had to join the family business of pencil-making. During 1837 and 1838, Thoreau attended a few sessions of the Transcendental Club and came in contact with some renowned persons of the time like Bronson Alcott, Margaret Fuller, William Henry Channing, Nathaniel Hawthorne and Horace Greeley. The most important event in this period was Thoreau's meeting with R.W.Emerson who had moved in to Concord. His contact with Emerson, the leading figure of the Transcendental movement, opened a new chapter in his life. In 1838, he opened a private school along with his brother John, which for some time became a very influential institution. During this year he also started lecturing at the Concord Lyceum. In 1839, he went on a boat journey on Concord and Merrimack rivers, an account of which was later published in his first book *A Week On The Concord and Merrimack Rivers*. In 1840 the Transcendentalists, launched the journal *Dial* and Thoreau started contributing to it. In 1841, he was invited by Emerson to live in his (Emerson's) house to work as a handyman and a gardener. The year is extremely important for he found "a chance for fuller emotional life" by being introduced to the wealth of Oriental, especially Indian, literature, Emerson's rich library contained several books on India and Thoreau devoured them with zeal and enthusiasm. The influence of Indian books on his young mind (Thoreau was twenty four years then) was profound and it shaped the future course of his life. In Emerson's library, Thoreau read Hindu scriptures like the *Vedas*, the *Upaniṣads*, the *Bhagavad Gitā* and the *Laws of Manu*. Thoreau lived in Emerson's house till 1843, the year when he left for the Staten Island. In 1844, he returned home and joined the pencil industry. On July 4, 1845 he left for Walden and continued to stay there till September 6, 1847 and came back to Emerson's house for his second residence. The remaining years of his life, till his death on May 6, 1862, were marked by such events as the publication of *A Week*, and his essay, "Civil Disobedience," *Walden*, and his anti-slavery movement, and his support for John Brown. During this period he visited Cape Cod, Canada, Maine Woods and Monadnock. Towards the last years of his life, he met Walt Whitman and John Brown.

As I have stated earlier, Thoreau had no knowledge of Indian scriptures during his college days. Though there were one or two references to the East, such as to Persian writing and Confucious in the college essays which he wrote during his Harvard days, his real interest in the East, especially India, began after he came to stay with Emerson. Both Franklin Benjamin Sanborn, the biographer of the Transcendentalists and Bartholow V. Crawford agree that Thoreau had no knowledge of India during his college days and the years that followed immediately. It was Emerson who aroused in him a true enthusiasm for India. Emerson and Thoreau came to know each other in 1837 and Emerson who was at that time immersed in his study of Indian scriptures drew Thoreau's attention to them. Four years later when Thoreau came to stay with Emerson, and had an access to his splendid library, he began to read some important Indian scriptures like the *Laws of Manu*, the *Bhagavad Gitā* and the *Upaniṣads* which he called the "Bibles of India." His journal enteries after 1841 bear strong evidence of his attraction to Indian scriptures and his wide reading of them. Two other periods during which he had an opportunity to read Indian scriptures are: 1849 to 1854 when he borrowed a large number of Indian scriptures from the Harvard University Library, and the year 1855 when his English friend Thomas Chilmondeley sent him a gift of 44 Oriental books which contained such titles as the *Rig Veda Samhita*, and *Mandukya Upanishads*, the *Vishnu Purana*, the *Institutes of Menu*, the *Bhagavat Geeta*, and the *Bhagavata Purana*'etc. Some of the important books he borrowed from the Harvard University Library were the *Mahabharata, Harwansa*, the *Sankhya karika*, the *Samved Samhita* the *Sacontala, or the Fatal Ring* and the *Bhagavat Geeta* etc. William Bysshe Stein has prepared a scholarly bibliography of Hindu and

Buddhist texts which Thoreau had read till 1854. The list contains 71 titles with an impressive selection of books containing many branches of Indian scriptures and literature such as the *Vedas*, the epics and *Puranas*, the *Kavyas*, the story literature (*Katha*), the dramas, grammar, the *Dharmasastras* and *Smrtis*, philosophy and religion, Buddhist and other vernacular texts.[6]

Thoreau was introduced to Indian scriptures by reading the *Laws of Menu* or *Manu Samhitā* as it is known in India. It had a profound influence on time. Immediately after reading the book in 1841, he made an entry in his Journal: "The impression which those sublime sentences made on me last night has awakened me before any cockcrowing."[7] He has recorded his impression of this book extensively and in many contexts. The book impressed on him the doctrine of detachment, renuciation and the need for solitude for a seeker of truth. The following passages taken from Thoreau's various writings suggest his admiration for the *Laws of Manu*: "I know of no book which comes to us with grander pretensions than the "Laws of Menu": and this immense presumption is so impersonal and sincere that it is never offensive or ridiculous. Observe the modes in which modern literature is advertised, and then consider this Hindoo prospectus. Think what a reading public it addresses, what criticism it expects. What wonder if the times were not ripe for it?"[8]

"The "Laws of Menu" are a manual of private devotion, so private and domestic and yet so public and universal a word as is not spoken in the parlour or pulpit in these days. It is so impersonal that it exercises our sincerity more than any other. It goes with us into the yard and into the chamber, and is yet later spoken than the advice of our mother and sisters."[9]

"The sublime sentences of Menu carry us back to a time when purification and sacrifice and self devotion had a place in the faith of men, and were not as now a superstition. They contain a subtle and refined philosophy also, such as in these times is not accompanied with so lofty and pure a devotion."[10]

The *Vedas* also impressed him in the like manner:

"What extracts from the Vedas I have read fall on me like the light of a higher and purer luminary, which describes a loftier course through a purer-stratum, - free from particulars, simple, universal. It rises on me like the full moon after the stars have come out, wading through some far summer stratum of the sky.... The Vedas contain a sensible account of God. The religion and philosophy of the Hebrews are those of a wilder and ruder tribe, wanting the civility and intellectual refinements and subtlety of the Hindoos. Man flows at once to God as soon as the channel of purity, physical, intellectual and moral is open."[11]

"The veneration in which the Vedas are held is itself a remarkable fact. Their code embraced the whole moral life of the Hindoo, and in such a case there is no other truth than sincerity. Truth is such by reference to the heart of man within, not to any standard without."[12]

In the chapter on Emerson, I have shown how the *Bhagavad Gitā* had greatly influenced and shaped the philosophy of Emerson. Its impact on Thoreau was no less, although the nature of that impact was different. Thoreau read the *Bhagavad Gitā* in 1845 after reading the *Laws of Manu*. For him *Bhagavad Gitā* was much greater thing than "all the ruins of the East."[13] What appealed to Thoreau in the *Bhagavad Gitā* was the philosophy of *niskāma Karma* or action without attachment and he learnt from it now to give up one's desire. His books - *A Week* and *Walden*-and his *Journals* are full of Vedic statements and paraphrased ideas from the *Gitā* regarding detachment. He also published a number of fine abstracts from various Hindu scriptures in the various issues of the *Dial*. In *Walden*, he writes: "I bathe my intellect in the stupendous and cosmogonal philosophy of the Bhagavat Gitā."[14] Recommending the *Bhagavad Gitā* to Americans, he writes in *A Week*: "I would say to the readers of the Scriptures, if they wish for a good book, read the Bhagavat Geeta, an episode to the Mahabharat... translated by Charles Wilkins. It deserves to be read with reverence even by Yankees, as a part of the sacred writings of a devout people: and the intelligent Hebrew will rejoice to find in it a moral grandeur and sublimity akin to those of his own scriptures."[15]

Thoreau, like other Transcendentalists, had a breadth and catholicity of mind which brought him to the study of religions of the Orient. From the beginning he was disillusioned with organised Christianity (he never went to the Church) and like Emerson he showed great interest in Hinduism and its philosophy. He confessed his lack of knowledge of Hebraism and his love for Eastern scriptures in *A Week*: "The reading which I love best is the scriptures of the several nations, though it happens that I am better acquainted with those of the Hindoos, the Chinese, and the Persians, than of the Hebrews."[16] The serenity and contemplative nature of Hinduism appealed to him most. In comparison to Hebraism, Thoreau found Hinduism superior in many ways. The following passage demonstrates Thoreau's disenchantment with

Hebraism, and his love for Hinduism: "The Hindoos are more serenely and thoughtfully religious than the Hebrews. They have perhaps a purer, more independent and impersonal knowledge of God. Their religious books describes the first inquisitive and contemplative access to God; the Hebrews bible a conscientious return, a grosser and more personal repentance. Repentance is not a free and fair highway to God. A wise man will dispense with repentance. It is shocking and passionate. God prefers that you approach him thoughtful, not penitent, though you are the chief of sinners. It is only by forgetting yourself that you draw near to him. The calmness and gentleness with which the Hindoo philosophers approach and discourse on forbidden themes is admirable."[17]

The Christian and Hindu concept of man, Thoreau thinks, are diametrically opposed to each other; the former sees man as a born sinner whereas the later takes him to be potentially divine. The lofty concept of man embodied in Hinduism appealed to Thoreau. Praising such a concept he writes: "In the Hindoo scriptures the idea of man is quite illimitable and sublime. There is nowhere a loftier conception of his destiny. He is at length lost in Brahma himself 'the divine male'. Indeed, the distinction of races in this life is only the commencement of a series of degrees which ends in Brahma."[18]

The influencing of Hinduism had a different effect on Thoreau than what it had on Emerson. Emerson, as we have seen earlier, took the intellectual and philosophical concepts such as the concepts of Over-Soul, *Māyā*, Law of *Karma* and rebirth etc. as refreshing concepts which expanded his vision of life, but Thoreau took the Hindu ideals of spiritual life and applied them to his own life. For him, the practical ideals such as renunciation, detachment, need for solitude, etc. had precedence over the abstract and speculative ideas mentioned above. As Carl T Jackson says: "Thoreau's response was more general and less intellectual...The concept of an all-embracing God-head or of a self punishing justice, which won Emerson's intellectual appreciation, were largely lost on his younger friend."[19] It may be made clear that though the abstract concepts were lost on Thoreau on the intellectual level they saturated his whole life, making the impact more radical. While in Emerson it remained on the level of belief and intellect, in Thoreau it was translated into daily action. My purpose is to show that in certain ways Thoreau went beyond his mentor and in certain other ways complemented him. The influence of India on Thoreau was complex and not so straightforward as it was on Emerson. Thus a mere comparison of passages from Thoreau, containing Hindu ideas with Hindu scriptures, having parallel ideas, will not be enough. The impact of Hindu scriptures has not only changed Thoreau's thought and vision, but has also directed his life's activities by orienting him to a way of life which is typically Indian. It has resulted in a character which is unAmerican in many ways and which is closer to a detached Hindu Yogi. So to understand Thoreau one has to study both his life and his writings.

Those who have tried to assess the nature of the Indian influence on Thoreau have come to the conclusion that Thoreau, more than Emerson, came closely to follow the Indian doctrines of liberation and translated them into action in his own life in the same way the Indian yogis did. Critics like Arthur Christy, Frank MacShane and Willaim Bysshe Stein have seen him as a Yogi. William Bysshe Stein in his two articles, "Thoreau's First Book: A Spoor of Yoga,"[20] and "Thoreau's *A Week* and *Om*

Cosmography"[21] shows similarity between soul's journey to eternity (the metaphor being that of a river merging into the sea) and Thoreau's symbolic journey in *A Week*. The route that *Jivātman* or individual soul takes to reach the *Paramātmān* or Universal Soul, Stein argues, has a symbolic correspondence with the structure of *A Week*. Stein juxtaposes the passages from the *Brahman Sutras* and *Yoga Sutras* with those from *A Week* to demonstrate the correspondence: "*A Week on Concord and Merrimack Rivers* offers a nineteenth century version of the Hindu itinerary of the divine journey (devayana) to spiritual liberation. A symbolic account of Thoreau's gradual mastery of yoga, the work evinces his disdain of all empirical knowledge, though particularly of Western historicism and its assumption of evolutionary progress. His familiarity with the various modalities of the quest for self-enlightenment is not a matter of speculation. In his *journal*, essays, and two completed books he constantly quotes from the Hindu religious writings devoted to the elucidation of the subject. However, his execution of *A Week* indicates that he also considers the doctrines of Buddhism as affirmations of the validity of the undertaking."[22]

Stein divides Thoreau's journey into four stages: waking dream (Saturday, Sunday, Monday); waking sleep (Tuesday, Wednesday); in dream awake (Wednesday,Thursday) and awaking of the true self (Friday). In another article "The Hindu Matrix of Walden: The King's Son,"[23] he further elucidates the nature and extent of the Indian influence on Thoreau. Frank MacShane's article "Walden and Yoga."[24] like Stein's, discusses *Walden* in the light of yoga. MacShane writes: "Certainly there is no doubt that the book is permeated with a vaguely Hindu atmosphere. There are many overt references to the sacred texts of India....And Thoreau himself follows certain Hindu customs:...There are also many less obvious references as for example to the language of silence which is so common in India and which is invoked in Thoreau's silent communion with the old fisherman who joined him at the pond."[25] The influence of Hinduism, MacShane seems to suggest, made Thoreau a *Yogi*. Thoreau himself said in a letter to H.G.O. Blake in 1849 his concept of a *Yogi*: "Free in this world as the birds in the air, disengaged from every kind of chains, those who have practised the *Yoga* gather in Brahmin the certain fruit of their works. Depend upon it that, rude and careless as I am, I would fain practice the *Yoga* faithfully. This yogi, absorbed in contemplation, contributes in his degree to creation; he breathes a divine perfume, he hears woderful things. Divine forms traverse him without tearing him and, united to the nature which is proper to him, he goes, he acts as animating original matter. To some extent, and at rare intervals, even I am a Yogi."[26]

While Stein studies Thoreau as a *Jnāna yogin*, MacShane studies him as a *Karma yogin*. Thoreau was also a *Raja Yogin*, an idea which critics have not touched upon. In fact, what I propose to do in the following pages is to study him as a composite Yogi who on different levels has emphasized different aspects of Yoga, such as *Jnāna* (knowledge), *karma* (action) and spiritual discipline in the line of *astānga yoga* (eight-fold method) of Patanjali. Thoreau's expansion of consciousness through knowledge earns him the title of *Jnāna yogi*, and his following of the principles of detached action and his 'Phalatrushnā vairāgya' or renouncement of the fruit of action make him a *karma yogin*.

His lifestyle characterised by *tapasyā* (austerites), his hatred of materialism, commercialism and industrialism (*Vishayan nindā*); his life of poverty; his love of solitude; his *Vairāgya* or asceticism; his practice of *ahimsā* and vegetarianism; his yogi-state of contentment; his description of his own trance-like states (akin to *samādhi*); his institutionalgrasp of the music of the universe akin to the mystical sound of *Om* (or *AUM*); his withdrawal from society and acceptance of fate; his lack of worldly ambition in life, all these bring him very close to the Hindu ascetic.

Yoga is one of the six orthodox Indian philosophical systems which is chiefly understood as a method of mental, spiritual and physical discipline ultimately leading to the *unio mystica* or the mystic union of the human Soul with the Universal Soul. Its esoteric method lies in arousing of the dormant spiritual energy in human beings and enabling an individual to function on the profoundest level of consciousness. There are various kinds of *Yoga* such as *Raja yoga, hatha yoga, jnāna yoga, karma yoga, laya yoga, montra yoga, dhyāna yoga, kriyā yoga, tantra yoga* and *japa yoga* etc. of these the three are most important: *jnāna yoga, karma yoga* and *raja yoga*.

Jnāna yoga or the way of knowledge is the most positive soteriological method of Hinduism. From the days of the *Upaniṣadas* and the *Bhagavad Gitā* to the time of Sankarāchārya it has been constantly emphasized as the royal road to liberation. In the *Bhagavad Gitā*, 'jnāna' has been regarded as the most sacred means of liberation!

na hi jñānena sadṛaśaṁ
pavitram iha vidyate
tat svayaṁ yagasaṁsiddhaḥ
kālenā 'tmani vindati.

> [Verily there is no purifier in this world like knowledge. He that is perfected in yoga realizes it in his own heart in due time.][27]

Through knowledge a religious man frees himself from the cycle of rebirth. According to the *Gitā*, the opposite of knowledge is doubt. One who has doubt, in the sense that one suspects true knowledge, is bound to be doomed. Therefore, the *Gitā* warns: "The ignorant, the man devoid of sraddha, the doubting self, goes to destruction. The doubting self has neither this world, nor the next, nor happiness."[28] As a Transcendentalist, Thoreau rejected the Lockean idea that true knowledge is available through one's senses. Instead, he accepted the Upaniṣadic idea that knowledge is available through supra-sensuous agencies. There are many instances where Thoreau shows his acceptance of such a view. On one occasion he remarks: "My genius makes distinctions which my understanding cannot, and which my senses do not report."[29] It is the knowledge of the nature of one's own individual soul and the universal soul that gives rise to freedom. The *Upaniṣads* insist that the individual soul and the universal soul are one and the same. *Jiva* is not different from *parama* or as the *Upaniṣads* says, *Tatvamasi*, Thou art that. This idea, it seems, appealed to Thoreau very much. In his Transcendental experience he must have realised this highest knowledge. The idea that the Universal Soul or Over-Soul is within oneself appealed to him most: "There is something proudly thrilling in the thought that this obedience to conscience and trust in God, which is so solemnly preached in extremities and arduous circumstances, is only to retreat to one's self, and rely on our own strength."[30] The Hindu as well as the Buddhist maxim *atmodeepobhava*, or be a lamp onto thyself, embodies such a concept. Thoreau wrote in his *journal* in 1856: "It is by obeying the suggestions of a higher light within you that you escape from yourself and ... travel totally new paths."[31] The objects of the phenomenal world, Thoreau seems to suggest, have manifold shapes and sizes but behind their multiplicity there is one divine spirit which gives life to them all. The familiar 'Vedāntic' example comes to one's mind. There may be water pots of various sizes but when they are placed outside, one sun reflects on all of them. Spiritual knowledge enables one to see unity in multiplicity. Thoreau expresses thus this typical Hindu concept: "The snow falls on no two trees alike, but the forms it assumes are as various as those of the twigs and leaves which receive it. They are predetermined, as it were by the genius of the tree. So one divine spirit descends alike on all, but bears a peculiar fruit in each. The divinity subsides on all men, as the snowflakes settle on the fields and ledges and takes the form of the various clefts and surfaces on which it lodges."[32] The chapters in *Walden* such as "Higher Laws" and "Sounds" contain many accounts of his Transcendental spiritual experiences which are similar to the experiences of a *jnāna yogin*. Thoreau's mystical vision of Transcendental reality appears to be somewhat akin to the Vedic seer's utterance: *Vedāhametam purusa mahantam* etc. In Thoreau's mystic vision of reality, time and space are transcendended and an oceanic feeling of total unity is poetically realised. He writes:

> Then Idle Time ran gadding by
> And left me with Eternity alone;
> I hear beyond the range of sound,
> I see beyond the verge of sight,-
> I see, smell, taste, hear, feel,
> That everlasting something
> To which we are allied,

At once our maker, our abode, our destiny,
Our very Selves....[33]

Besides the *Laws of Manu*, the other Indian scripture which profoundly influenced Thoreau was the *Bhagavad Gitā* which he called the Bible of the Hindus. The central teaching of the *Bhagavad Gitā* is the principle of *anāsakta karma*, i.e. action without attachment. This principle appealed to Thoreau immensely, and he wanted to model his life according to it. Frank Macshane says that Thoreau consistently followed the path of action propounded in the *Bhagavad Gitā*. Sri Krishna in the *Bhagavad Gitā* urges Arjuna to act without any attachment. Arjuna, who could not renounce his secular duties of a *kshyatriya* was hero, was asked to perform his duty without waiting for the fruit of his labour. Action performed in this manner frees one from the *kārmic* circuit; hence such action is free from any *karma phala*, or fruit of action. Its other implication is that such a way of salvation does not require an individual to renounce his worldly duties and retire to a forest to contemplate the *Brahman*. Such a method is called *Karma Yoga* as it is characterized by normal participation in one's everyday activities. What one is required to do is to detach oneself not from the acts but from their results.

This teaching of *Karma yoga* of the *Bhagavad Gitā* is an important Hindu contribution to the method of salvation of a worldly person. In the words of Mircea Eliade, "This interpretation of yoga technique, which presents it as an instrument permitting man to detach himself from the world while yet continuing to live and act in it, is characteristic of the magnificent synthetic effort of the author of the *Bhagavad Gitā*, which sought to reconcile all vocations (ascetic, mystical, active) as it had reconciled Vedantic monism with Samkhya pluralism."[34]

Thoreau saw in the doctrine of *karma yoga* of the *Bhagavad Gitā* something highly instructive. The idea appealed to him because he was struggling to become a contemplative saint without avoiding action. One of the cardinal points of the Emerson philosophy was the need for significance of action in life. Emerson chided Thoreau for not being sufficiently active. Emerson perhaps could not understand Thoreau's action based on *karma yoga*. W.E. Nagley suggests that Thoreau always sought to reconcile contemplation with action, which appeared to be two irreconcilable opposites: "When Thoreau struggled with the tension between his desire to act significantly and his wish for serenity, he was wrestling with a problem that has been solved by a non-attached person, who acts significantly without attachment and with serenity."[35] This dilemma and struggle on Thoreau's part, as one can see, are expressed clearly in *A Week*: "But how can I communicate with the gods, who am I a pencil-maker on the earth and not be insane?"[36] Luckily, Thoreau found the solution in the *Gitā* which he found more instructive than even Shakespeare: "In comparison with the philosophers of the East we may say that modern Europe has yet given birth to none. Beside the vast and cosmogonal philosophy of the Bhagavad-Geeta, even our Shakespeare seems sometimes youthfully green and practical merely."[37] In *A Week*, he liberally and approvingly quotes such verses from Sir Charles Wilkins' translation which embody the principle of *Karma yoga:*

> The man enjoyeth not freedom from action, ... nor doth he obtain happiness from a total inactivity. No one ever resteth a moment inactive .... The man who

> restraineth his active faculties, and sitteth down with his mind attentive to the objects of his senses, is called one of an astrayed soul, and the practicer of deceit. So the man is praised, who, having subdued all his passions, performeth with his active faculties all the functions of life, unconcerned about the event.
>
> Let the motive be in the deed and not in the event. Be not one whose motive for action is the hope of reward. Let not thy life be spent in inaction.
>
> For the man who doeth that which he hath to do, without affection, obtaineth the Supreme.
>
> x x x
>
> He [the wise man] abandoneth the desire of a reward of his actions; he is always contented and independent; and although he may be engaged in a work, he as it were doeth nothing.[38]

Thoreau's whole life can be regarded as an experiment in the line of *anāskta karmayoga* of the *Bhagavad Gitā*. The Walden experiment can be seen as an effort in this direction. There are many passages in *Walden,* including the chapter called "Higher Laws," which clearly suggest detached action. In *A Week,* Thoreau also writes about detachment: "But they who are unconcerned about the consequences of their actions, are not therefore unconcerned about their action."[39] Throughout his life he had lived without aspiring to any fruit of action, in whatever he did he was being propelled by a sense of duty. In the chapter called "The Bean Field" he laughs at the farmers who are solely guided by the idea of profit and, therefore, are trammelled by the fruit of action. Thoreau was never affected by the conflict of success and failure. Like a true yogi, he never had any personal ambition. Lewis Mumford remarks: "In a period when men were on the move, he remained still; when men were on the make, he remained poor...."[40] He was perhaps the only man of leisure in Concord at that time who had personally nothing to "achieve." The only thing that he wanted through disinterested action and contemplation was an authentic vision of reality. He would reflect: "What, after all, does the practicalness of life amount to? The things immediate to be done are very trivial. I could postpone them all to hear this locust sing. The most glorious fact in my experience is not anything that I have done or may hope to do, but a transient thought, or vision, or dream, which I have had. I would give all the wealth of the world and all the deeds of all the heroes, for one true vision."[41] Thoreau was not a "prisoner of his necessity," and because he understood "the activities" in order to sit down to listen to the song of the locust.

I have suggested earlier that more than a *jnāna yogi* or *karma yogi* Thoreau was a *raja yogi* or a yogi understood in Patanjali's sense. His austere programme at Walden is very much like the way of a *yogi*. His love of solitude, withdrawal from society, hatred of materialism, frugal living, austerities, *ahimsā* and vegetarianism and his experience of *Samādhi* are some of the aspects of his yogi-like existence. Though Thoreau never followed the rigid steps of yoga prescribed by Patanjali, he was a yogi in a broad way. Charles R. Anderson rightly says: "The actual discipline of yoga was used by Thoreau in a deliberately loose way, simply as the ascetic gesture of one deeply drawn to the Oriental scriptures."[42] Arthur Christy says:

"Of course the word *Yogi* suggests certain very definite things that Thoreau never intended."[43] Christy has, in mind Moncure Conway's concept of a yogi described thus: "Like the pious Yogi, so long motionless whilst gazing on the sun that knotty plants encircled his neck and the cast snake-skin his loins, and the birds built their nests on his shoulders, this poet and naturalist, by equal consecration, became a part of the field and forest."[44] What Conway says about a *yogi* is no doubt, a superficial description. *Yoga* creates an expansion of consciousness leading ultimately to the experience of essential oneness of the univese, in a state of *Samādhi*. What Conway describes are certain external ascetic practices which are practised by mendicants. Thoreau was practising *yoga* in a broad way, not in a narrow and restricted sense, described by Conway. He accepted the essentials and rejected its superficiality. As we shall shortly see, he practised consciously or unconsciously some of the basic tenets of *astāngayoga*. As the *Bhagavad Gitā* says: "A Yogi should always try to concentrate his mind living alone in solitude, having subduedh his mind and body and get rid of desires and possessions."[45] His experiment at Walden was mad in the spirit of a seeker of truth, a *banāprasthin* who goes to the forest to cast off the superflux of life and to realise the truth. Thoreau declares in the beginning of *Walden:* "I went to the woods because I wished to live deliberately, to front only the essential facts of life, and see if I could not learn what it had to teach, and not, when I came to die, discover that I had not lived. I did not wish to live what was not life, living is so dear nor did I wish to practise resignation, unless it was quite necessary. I wanted to live deep and suck out all the marrow of life, to live so sturdily and Spartan-like as to put to rout all that was not life, to cut a broad swath and shave close, to drive life into a corner, and reduce it to its lowest terms, and if it proved to be mean, why then to get the whole and genuine meanness of it, and publish its meanness to the world; or if it were sublime, to know it by experience, and be able to give a true account of it ...."[45]

This solemn declaration is very significant. The aim of this experiment is not simply to write a book in solitude. It suggests a grand spiritual project of a *yogi*, a life of *tapasyā* or tranquil meditation. *Tapasyā* is associated with creation, and so Thoreau went to the Walden pond to create and be a poet and know his own identity. Thoreau's concept of *Yoga*, thus, has something to do with the act of creation. It is akin to Patanjali's concept. Patanjali describes it as "a methodical effort to attain perfection, through the control of the different elements of human nature, physical and psychical ...."[46] Thoreau's main interest was "not metaphysical theorising, but the practical motive of indicating how salvation can be attained by disciplined activity."[47]

According to Patanjali, the method of *Yoga* consists of eight stops such as *Yamaniyamāsanap-ranāyamapratyāhāradharanādhyanasamādhayoastavan-gani*. Or "abstentions and observances and postures and regulations-of-the-breath and withdrawl-of-the-senses and fixed attention and contemplation and concentration are the eight aids."[48] In Patanjali's *Yogasūtras* there are various methods of *Yoga* like the following. They are *ahimsā* (non-violence), *satya* (truthfulness), *āsteya* (none covetousness), *brahmacharya* (continence), *aparigraha* (frugal living), *shaucha* (physical and mental purity), *santosa* (contentment), *tapas* (austrities), *swadhya* (study of scriptures) and *Ishwarapranidhāna* (total dedication to God).

Thoreau practised, more or less, all the methods of *Yoga* except perhaps the practice of breath control or the regulations of the breath. His great regard for animal life, his early conservationist attitude and his vegetarianism were aspects of *ahimsā*, his lack of material ambition was an aspect of *āsteya*, his frugal living was *aparigraha*, his bachelorhood was continence. His life was a life of austorities (tapasyā) and contentment (santosa). His *swadhya* was his reading of a large number of Indian religious scriptures. Though Thoreau did not practise any particular *yogic asanā* (posture) he sat in many meditative postures while living in his hut in Walden and this subscribes to Patanjali's liberal view of *āsana-Stherasukhamāsanam*.[49] He practised *pratyāhāra* in his withdrawal from luxury and many fleeting pleasures of life. His withdrawal from society can also be viewed as an act of *pratyāhāra*. *Dhāranā* and *dhyāna* are practised by him in a very broad way. He established himself in *Satvaguna* and his many morning and evenings were spent in Walden in meditation. There is at least one instance in Walden which describes a trance-like state akin to the beatific experience of *Samādhi*.

As I have said earlier, the two books which profoundly influenced Thoreau were the *Laws of Manu* and the *Bhagavad Gitā*. The verses of Manu which were chosen for the *Dial* of 1843 aroused Thoreau's interest in *yoga* and solitude. The verses were: "A Brahmin should constantly shun worldly honour, as he would shun poison; and rather constantly seek disrespect as he would seek nectar."[50] "Alone, in some solitary place, let him constantly meditate on the divine nature of the soul, for, by such meditation he will obtain happiness."[51] "Alone let him constantly dwell, for the sake of his own felicity; observing the happiness of a solitary man, who neither forsakes nor is forsaken, let him live without a companion."[52] Manu has put the matter more specifically in the following two verses where the essential lonliness of man is described in the manner of existentialism: "Single is each man born; single he dies; single he receives the reward of his good, and single the punishment of his evil deeds," and "When he leaves his corpse, like a log or a lump of clay, on the ground, his kindred retire with averted faces, but his virtue accompanies his soul."[53] The *Bhagavad Gitā* also lays great emphasis on the need for solitude for a *sādhaka*. For yoga solitude is the prime requisite. The *Gitā* is very explicit in this matter: "A yogi should always try to concentrate his mind living alone in solitude, having subdued his mind and body and got rid of desires and possessions. Having firmly fixed in a clean place, his seat, neither too high nor too low, and having spread over it the kusa-grass, a deer skin and a cloth, one over the other; sitting there on his seat, making the mind one-pointed and restraining the thinking faculty and the senses, he should practise yoga for self-purification."[54] It must be clarified here that initially Thoreau's love of solitude had nothing to do with his reading of the *Laws of Manu* or the *Bhagavad Gitā*. It was innate in him and was only intensified by his reading of these Indian scriptures. His early interest in solitude, which was perhaps the romantic interest of a young poet, was transformed and consolidated as the very basic need of a seeker of truth. In a most significant statement Thoreau said: "I have an immense appetite for solitude, like an infant for sleep."[55] The Walden experience was primarily a search for solitude for the purpose of spiritual *sādhanā*. Chapters like "Solitude" "Sound" and "Visitors" explore at length the problem and the need for solitude. Throughout the book solitude works as leitmotiv. "As the truest society approaches always nearer to solitude, so the most excellent speech finally falls into Silence .... Silence .... is when we hear inwardly, sound when we hear outwardly ... Who has not hearkened to her infinite din? She is Truth's speaking -trumpet... through her all revelations have been made."[56] In several journal entries he has expressed similar attitudes. Thoreau's going to Walden is seen by Anderson as symbolic of a spiritual rebirth. Commenting on a significant sentence from his journal (such as "You think that I am impoverishing myself by withdrawing from men, but in my solitude I have woven for myself a silken web or *Chrysalis,* and, nymph-like, shall ere long burst forth a more perfect creature, fitted for a higher society,)"[57] he writes: "His [Thoreau's] withdrawal was a preparation for rebirth, since it enabled him to complete his development from the nymph or pupa stage, the highest ever reached by most men."[58] In solitude, Thoreau became truly creative and contemplative. He shunned visitors and devoted his time to simple work and meditation. Solitude helped him to be a true *yogi*. He said at one point: "I thrive best on solitude".

Withdrawal from society is just another aspect of solitude. The *Gitā* says that a *yogi* should live alone in the forest and develop a distaste for the society of men (*aratirjnasansadi*). One who practises yoga becomes, in a sense, anti-social and its extreme form (as in Tantra) antinomian. In Eliade's words the method of yoga "comprises a number of different techniques (physiological, mental, mystical), but they all have one characteristic in common -- they are antisocial, or, indeed, antihuman. The worldly man lives in society, marries, establishes a family; Yoga prescribes absolute solitude and chastity."[59] Thoreau was called a misanthropist for his hatred of society. He writes in *Walden:* "My purpose in going to Walden Pond was not to live cheaply nor to live dearly there, but to transact some private business with the fewest obstacles."[60] The obstacles include the intrusion of men. Truly, he wanted to pursue his own private life and its goals. Danial Ricketson, a New Bedford Quaker and a sincere admirer of Thoreau, was appalled by Thoreau's anti-social stance. Thoreau in his letter to Ricketson wrote: "Why will you waste so many regards on me, and not know what to think of my silence? Infer from it what you might from the silence of a dense pine wood.... My silence is just as inhuman as that, and no more. You know that I never promised to correspond with you, and so, when I do, I do more than I promised.... life is short, and there are other things also to be done. I admit that you are more social than I am, and far more attentive to 'the common courtesies of life' but this is partly for the reason that you have fewer or less exacting private pursuits."[61]

Like his contempt for society, Thoreau's contempt for materialism and his embracing of poverty are also well known. Here, the influence of Indian scriptures is clearly discernible. Transcendental philosophy also contributed to this. His going to Walden, as we have noted, was to reduce his wants to the minimum. This can be seen as a true yogic ideal. To quote Anderson," ... his first gambit is to slay the dragon Materialism that was plaguing the Americans of his time."[62] Thoreau's entire life was geared towards that goal to oppose the demon of materialism. He always sneered at the rich: "The luxuriously rich are not simply kept comfortably warm, but unnaturally hot; as I implied before, they are cooked, of course *a La mode*."[63] His contempt for the luxury of the rich was framed in unmistakable terms in many contexts of his writings. Like a true Indian sage, he would say: "I would rather sit on a pumpkin and have it all to myself than be crowded on a velvet cushion,"[64] and "Cultivate poverty like a garden herb, like sage ..... It is life near the bone, where it is sweetest .... superfluous wealth can buy superfluities only. Money is not required to buy one necessary of the soul."[65] His love of poverty prompted many to call him a penurious fanatic, but his poverty made him an "essential" man. "Simplify, simplify, simplify" was his motto. This philosophy he learnt both from the Unitarians, and the *Manu Samhitā* and the *Bhagavad Gitā*. His doctrine of simplicity, Leo Stoller says, aims at measuring "men and economies,... the most complete realization of the perfectibility innate in every person. The man who strives for it is not trying to find the way to wealth but the way to invent and get a patent for himself."[66] His life of simplicity and poverty and lack of any worldly ambition can be best compared with the Hindu ideal of *vairāgya* (stoic indifference) and *santosa* (contentment). His frugal living also is the realization of the ideal of *aparigraha*.

Thoreau's criticism of industrialism and mechinery is related to his contempt for materialism and commercialism. He was almost a pioneer in reflecting upon the miscry that industrialism and machine civilization was to bring. He had before him writers like Rousseau and Wordsworth and anticipated such stern critics of machine civilization as Tolstoy, Henry Adams, Lewis Mumford, Edward Dahlberg and Thomas Merton. He could clearly visualize the consequences of dissociating oneself from nature and turning towards machines. He also visualized man becoming just another object among many objects, and a cog in the big wheel of universal machine. His ideal, as we know, was a life of harmony with nature, and not a life in the city. Like Wordsworth, he was a harsh critic of the railways.

Thoreau's doctrine of simplicity is demonstrated very well in the nature of his food. As we already know, Thoreau was a staunch vegetarian. In America the vegetarian movement was started by an English man Rev. William Metcalfe who migrated to America in 1817, the year of, Thoreau's birth. Metcalfe wrote the first tract on vegetarianism in America and later edited *The American Vegetarianism.* A connection can be established between Metcalfe's and Thoreau's vegetarianism. Metcalfe converted Dr. William A. Alcott to vegetarianism, and later Dr. Alcott's cousin Amos Bronson Alcott (a minor transcendentalist) accepted vegetarianism. As Bronson Alcott was Thoreau's friend he became an exemplar for Thoreau's vegetarianism. Thoreau's vegetarianism can be seen as part of his *yogic sādhanā*. He was an animal conservationist and had great regard for the life of the animal. His vegetarianism started initially as a reaction against uncleanliness of animal food, and later became an important part of his austere life. He writes: "The practical objection to animal food in my case was its uncleanliness; and besides, when I had caught and cleaned and cooked and eaten my fish, they seemed not to have fed me essentially."[67] In another place he writes: "I have found repeatedly, of late years, that I cannot fish without falling a little in self-respect."[68] In *Walden,* Thoreau justifies vegetarianism thus "It appears from the above estimate, that my food alone cost me in money about twenty-seven cents a week. It was, for nearly two years after this, rye and Indian meal without yeast, potatoes, rice, a very little salt pork, molasses, and salt; and my drink, water. It was fit that I should live on rice, mainly, who loved so well the philosophy of India."[69]

His concept of *ahimsā* and vegetarianism which are tied with each other are influenced by Hinduism. By refraining himself from animal food Thoreau came very close to a Brahmin's lifestyle.

The last stage of Yoga in Patanjali's eight-step path or *astānga yoga* system called *samādhi* can be compared to Zen's satori and the Buddhist *nirvāna*. Samādhi is a state of mind without tension in which ecstasy and stasis are conjoined to produce beatitude. In Radhakrishnan's words, *Samādhi* "is the ecstatic condition in which the connection with the outer world is broken. It is the goal of the Yoga discipline, since it leaves the soul from its temporal, conditioned, changing existence into a simple, eternal and perfect life."[70] In this state, the individual soul or *jivātman* merges with the Over-Soul or *Paramātman* and no distinction between the seeker and the sought, the observer and the observed remains. It is a state of total unity and total bliss.

There are, of course, not many instances in Thoreau's writings, as in Emerson's to demonstrate that he is reaching the ecstatic trance-like state which can be regarded as *Samādhi*. There is only one key passage in *Walden,* often quoted by critics, which shows that there was a yogi in Thoreau who reached this much sought-after state. That Thoreau was temperamentally prone to such a beatific state can be seen from other instances also. Recalling his earlier visit to Walden, Thoreau describes incidents which bring him very close to the trance-like state. He writes: "I have spent many an hour, when I was younger, floating over its surface as the zephyr willed, ... dreaming awake, until I was aroused by the boat touching the sand, and I arose to see what shore my fates had impelled me to."[71] The trance-like state described above may not be compared fully with the state of *samādhi*. But the following paragraph would unmistakably show that the state is akin to the *Samādhi* of yoga. In the following paragraph Thoreau describes an ideal state of serenity which can be attained only by yoga: "Sometimes, in a summer morning, having taken my accustomed bath, I sat in my sunny doorway from sunrise till noon, rapt in a revery, amidst the pines and hickories and sumachs, in undisturbed solitude and stillness, while the birds sang around or flitted noiseless through the house, until by the sun falling in at my west window, or the noise of some traveller's wagon on the distant highway, I was remained of the lapse of time, I grew in those seasons like corn in the night, and they were far better than the work of the hands would have been. They were not time subtracted from my life, but so much over and above my usual allowance. I realized what the Orientals mean by contemplation and the forsaking of works."[72]

This passage reflects Thoreau's inclinations. Like a yogi, in his state of deep meditation, Thoreau was completely oblivious of the external world. The sense of time and space was completely lost for him. He was awakened only when there was some compelling distraction. It was only in retrospect that he was able to know how much time had elapsed. The state of *Samādhi* is a state of non-action. It is free from any gross element that action embraces. Thoreau clearly comprehends the meaning of such a state and compares it with the Oriental contemplation, *Samādhi*. The similarity of the experience described in the above passage with that of *Samādhi* prompts Christy to make the following observation: "The Hindu Yogi wrapt" in his contemplations is not a far cry from the picture Thoreau gives of himself, sitting in his sunny doorway lost in reverie, oblivious of time from sunrise till noon, oblivious even of the songs of birds."[73]

Closely allied to *Samādhi* is Thoreau's experience of listening to the cosmic sound which he has mentioned in various contexts. The *anāhata dhwani* described in *yoga* is a kind of cosmic sound whose vibration a yogi feels in his heart through his intuitive faculty. W.B. Stein has worked out in great detail how Thoreau has given us many instances in *A Week* of hearing the music of the Universe similar to the sound of *AUM*, the Hindu symbol of cosmic sound. To give one instance from Stein: "His subsequent elaboration of the ideas in this passage integrates the barking with two ceremonial aspects of heavenly light and with the yogic goal of perfect physical and mental control: 'All these sounds, the crowing of cocks, the baying of dogs, and the hum of insects at noon, are the evidence of nature's health or *sound* state (1, 40). But it is in the dissolution of 'wow' into 'wo', of 'wo' into ('w' and the 'W' into engulfing silence that he recaptures the essence of meditation on the mystical monosyllable *OM*."[74]

As an ecologist and a pioneer conservationist Thoreau loved nature. His collection of minute details relating to trees, birds and other aspects of nature places him in the rank of a scientist. Nature also helped him to become a poet. He wrote early in his journal that nature provided a setting for his dream: "That woodland vision for a long time made the drapery of my dreams."[75] Besides loving nature as a poet, Thoreau was attracted to nature in a special way, and this relates to his mystical temperament. He sought god in nature. He tells us that his idea behind going to Walden was not to live cheaply, but to transact some "private business." This "private business," one may suppose, was to see or realize God in nature. The Hindus say that the rivers and the seas are nothing but the body of God: *Saritsamudranchharesariram*. So Thoreau's love for nature can be seen as a part of his theological system which suggests that divinity resides in both the animate and the inanimate world. His transcendentalist friend, William Ellery Channing, called him "the poet-naturalist."[76] A. Bronson Alcott said that he had "the profoundest passion for nature of any one living."[77] Emerson also had many kind words to say about Thoreau's love of nature.

Thoreau's communion with nature, as I have suggested above, was on a mystical level. It was pantheistic in nature. His exploration of the world of nature was nothing but a metaphorical self-exploration. In his Walden experiment he withdrew from society in order to explore the inner recesses of his own soul indirectly through nature. Communion with nature was a transcendentalist requirement emphasized by Emerson and others. In the words of Crawford: "The desirability of communion with nature was one of the few articles of faith in which all Transcendentalists agreed. Instead of indulging in mere theory, Thoreau would be putting his belief into practice. At the same time he would be doing that he longed most to do."[78] In Walden, Thoreau felt merged with nature and by that with God. Whenever he was slightly distant from nature he always complained about it. His kinship with all objects of nature made him a kind of Vedāntin who has no separate entity outside the world of nature. The trees grow in him, the sun shines in him, the river and ocean flow in him. Sitting in his hut near Walden Thoreau had a similar experience. In another context, he describes such experience thus:

Fain would I stretch me
by the highway-side
To thaw and trickle
with the melting snow;
That mingled, soul and body,
with the tide,
I too may through
the pores of nature flow.[79]

One would be tempted to state here that Thoreau's Oriental nature and his experiment with simple living influenced one of the greatest Indians of all time, Mahatma Gandhi. That Gandhi was influenced by Thoreau is proof enough that Thoreau had something in him akin to the spirit of this great Indian. In Christy's words: "Mahatma Gandhi's adoption of Thoreau's principles is in itself the most definite proof that can be found of the latter's Oriental temper."[80] Gandhi and Thoreau had many things in common between them: both were believers in non-violence, both were vegetarians, both believed in "civil disobedience" or "passive resistance" and both were religious in temperament. Besides, both of them admired the teaching of the *Bhagavad Gitā* and wanted to live upto its ideal, and both appreciated poverty and lived very simple life, reducing their needs to the minimum.

We may conclude this chapter with this observation by Webb Miller: "Gandhi received back from America what was fundamentally the philosophy of India after it had been distilled and crystallized in the mind of Thoreau."[81] Thus, Indian philosophy and religion were so much assimilated by Thoreau that latter day saints like Gandhi went back to this great transcendentalist to receive inspiration.

Footnote:

1. Emerson, *Complete Works*, X, p. 457. (Thoreau)

2. John Burroughs, "Thoreau's Wildness," in *Thoreau: A Century of Criticism*, pp.87-90.

3. Havelock Elis, "Thoreau" in *Thoreau: A Century of Criticism*, pp. 91-96.

4. *Complete Works*, X, p. 452. (Thoreau)

5. Christy, *The Orient*, p. 188.

6. W. B. Stein, "A Bibliography of Hindu and Buddhist Literature Available to Thoreau through 1854," *ESQ*, 47, part 2 (11 Qtr., 1967), pp. 52-56.

7. Thoreau, *Journal*, I, 267.

8. Ibid., p. 264.

9. Ibid., p. 279.

10. Ibid., p. 280.

11. *Journal*, II, p.4.

12. *Journal* I, pp. 275-276.

13. Ibid. IV, P. 438.

14. *Writings*, II, p. 328 (Walden)

15. Ibid., I, pp. 147-148. (A week)

16. Ibid., p. 72.

17. *Journal*, II, p. 3.

18. *Journal*, I, p. 275.

19. Carl T. Jackson, p. 431.

20. W. B. Stein, "Thoreau's First Book: A Spoor of Yoga," *The Emerson Society Quarterly*, 41 (IV Qtr., 1965), 4-25.

21. Stein, "Thoreau's *A Week* and *Om* Cosmography," in *Artist and Citizen Thoreau*, ed. J.J. McAlean (Hartford: Transcendental Books, 1971), pp.15-37.

22. Ibid., p. 15.

23. Stein, "The Hindu Matrix of *Walden*: The King's Son," *Comparative Literature*, XXII, 3 (Summer, 1970), pp. 303-318.

24. Frank MacShane, "Walden and Yoga," *The New England Quarterly*, XXXVII, 3 (Sept., 1964), pp.322-342.

25. Ibid., pp. 322-323.

26. *Writings*, VI, p. 175.

27. *Bhagavad Gitā*, pp. 317-318 (IV:38)

28. Ibid., p. 320. (IV: 40)

29. *Journal*, II, p. 337.

30. Ibid., I, p. 180.

31. Ibid., IX, p. 38.

32. Ibid., I, p. 185.

33. *Writings*, I, pp. 181-182 (A Week)

34. Mircea Eliade, *Yoga: Immortality and Freedom*, tr. from French by Willard R. Trask (1958; rpt. New York: Princeton Univ. Press, 1970), pp. 158-159.

35. Winfield K. Nagley, "Thoreau on Attachment, Detachment, and Non-Attachment," *Philosophy East and West*, 111, 4 (Jan. 1954), p. 320.

36, *Writings*, I, p. 149. (A Week)

37. Ibid., p. 139.

38. Ibid., pp. 144-145.

39. Ibid., p.146.

40. Lewis Mumford, "From *The Golden Day*," in *Thoreau: A Collection of Critical Essays*, ed. Sherman Paul (N.J.: Prentice-Hall, Inc., 1962), p.13.

41. *Writings*, I, pp. 145-146. (A Week).

42. Charles R. Anderson, *The Magic Circle of Walden* (New York: Holt, Rinehart and Winston, 1968), p.87.

43. *The Orient*, p.207.

44. M.D. Conway, *Emerson at Home and Abroad* (Boston: James H. Osgood, 1882), p. 280.

45. *Writings*, II, pp. 100-101. (Welden)

46. *Indian Philosophy*, II, p. 338.

47. Ibid.

48. *The Yoga-System of Patanjali*, tr. James Houghton Woods (1914; rpt., Delhi:Motilal

Banarasidass, 1966), p. 177. (Yoga- Sūtras, II: 29)

49. Ibid., p. 191. (II: 46).

50. "The Laws of Manu," *The Dial* (New York: Russell and Russell, 1961), III, p 336.

51. Ibid., p. 337.

52. Ibid.

53. Ibid.

54. *Bhagavad Gitā*, pp. 368-371. (VI: 10-12)

55. Thoreau, *The Correspondence of Henry David Thoreau*, ed. W. Harding and Carl Bode (Washington: New York Univ. Press, 1958), p.493. (Sept. 9,1857).

56. *Writings*, I, pp. 418-419. (A Week)

57. *Journal*, IX, p. 246.

58. Anderson: *The Magic Circle*, p.57.

59. Eliade, p. 95.

60. *Writings*, II, p. 21 (Walden)

61. Thoreau, *Correspondence*, p.599.

62. Anderson, p. 19.

63. *Writings*, II, p. 15. (Walden)

64. Ibid., p. 41.

65. Ibid., pp. 361, 362.

66. Leo Stoller, "Thoreau's Doctrine of Simplicity" in *Thoreau: A Collection of Critical Essays*, p.37.

67. *Writings*, II, p. 237 (Walden).

68. Ibid., p. 236.

69. Ibid., p. 67.

70. *Indian Philosophy*, II, p. 358.

71. *Writings*, II, p. 213. (Walden).

72. Ibid., pp. 123-124.

73. *The Orient*, p. 221.

74. Stein, "Thoreau's *A Week and Om* cosmography," p.19.

75. Quoted by Carl Bode in *The Portable Thoreau* (1947; rpt. New York: The Viking Press, 1974), Intro. pp. 4-5.

76. W. E. Channing, *Thoreau: The Poetic-Naturalist* (1902; rpt. New York: Biblio and Tannen, 1966).

77. A. B. Alcott, "Thoreau" in *Thoreau: A Century of Criticism*, p. 57.

78. Crawford, p. XXX.

79. *Writings*, V, p. 409. (The Thaw)

80. *The Orient*, p.211.

81. Webb Miller, *I Found No Peace* (New York: The literary Guide, Inc., 1936), p. 240.

V

THE MINOR PROPHETS

At this stage, it is necessary to examine how and to what extent some of Emerson's and Thoreau's contemporaries, who contributed significantly to Transcendentalism, were influenced by the current of ideas flowing from the Orient. Unfortunately, minor transcendentalists, whose number in fact is legion, have not received the attention they deserved. They have been neglected by most critics, except perhaps Perry Miller who has given them some attention. A movement, in order to be a full-fledged movement, needs not only its leaders but also its supporters and sympathisers whose share to the whole movement can hardly be under rated. In this case, the major figures together with the minor ones given true character to the movement. Though the Transcendental movement of New England was local one, and its duration was brief compared to other movements, like the Renaissance or the Romantic movement, it left a deep mark on the history of American life and literature. The deep-rooted conviction of its members, has continued to influence other writers and alter the attitude of people, and hence the relevance of the movement. Politicians, moralists, social reformers, writers and the mystics in their own way continue to derive inspiration from Emerson and his colleagues.

A study of Transcendentalism, will not be complete without throwing some light on the figures who surrounded Emerson and Thoreau. These minor figures who contributed in various significant ways to the movement are: Amos Bronson Alcott (1799-1888), George Ripley (1802-1880), Theodore Parker (1810-1860), James Freeman Clarke (1810-1888), Samuel Johnson (1822-1882), Dr. William Ellery Channing (1780-1842), Orestes Brownson (1803-1876), Frederic Henry Hedge (1805-1890), [Sarah] Margaret Fuller (1810-1850), Christopher Cranch (1813-1892), Samuel Osgood (1813-1880), Jones Very (1813-1880), Samuel Longfellow (1819-1892), Octavious B. Frothingham (1822-1895), Thomas Wentworth Higginson (1823-1911), Franklin Benjamin Sanborn (1831-1917), Moncure Conway (1823-1907), Elizabeth Palmer Peabody (1804-1894) and William Henry Channing (1810-1884). Amos Bronson Alcott was a great teacher and populariser of Transcendental ideas; Margaret Fuller was the editor of *Dial*, the mouthpiece of the Transcendentals for the first two years; George Ripley was the founder of the famous Brook Farm Association, a utopian community organised as an experiment in community living; Elizabeth P. Peabody and Margaret Fuller were dynamic propagators of Transcendental ideas; Orestes Brownson was a powerful minister, editor, politician and novelist; James Freeman Clarke was, in his own way, a populariser of Oriental ideas among American readers and listeners and became influential through his book *Ten Great Religions* in which Hinduism was included; Samuel Johnson became known for his book *Oriental Religions And Their Relation to Universal Religion*; William Ellery Channing was inclined towards Orientalism and opposed

Calvinistic doctrines; Theodore Parker was a fiery agitator, a social reformer and a Unitarian clergyman who opposed the special authority of the *Bible;* Thomas Wentworth Higginson worked for the unity of religions and was influenced considerably by Buddhism and his edition of extracts from Max Muller's translation of *Dhammapada* is worth mentioning in this context; Jones Very was an Oriental mystic; Moncure Conway was perhaps the only member of the Transcendentalist group who made a pilgrimage to India and narrated the account of his visit in *My pilgrimage to the Wiseman of the East;* Frederic Henry Hedge had read a fairly large number of books on Orientalism; as the borrowing register of Harvard College shows; Orestes Brownson successfully defended Transcendentalism against the charges lavelled by Andrew Norton. Though the minor transcendentalists, mentioned above, appear to have made no substantial contribution to the movement individually, they have certainly made a large contribution as a group. Perry Miller has rightly pointed out that: "... even though the specific achievements of these writers were seldom of the very first order, yet the achievement of the group as a whole --even with Emerson and Thoreau hugely omitted-- remains a significant episode in the American experience."[1]

There are many reasons why the minor Transcendentalists are not studied properly. First, there is a dearth of material on them; secondly, these people were mainly social organisers, preachers, lecturers and conversationalists, and wrote very little. Some of their letters and journals and stray writings are still kept in dark and obscure corners of libraries. During their own time also some of them were not at all popular and their voice could not reach the critics. We now know by hindsight that to ignore them is to impair our full understanding of Transcendentalism. If Emerson and Thoreau are flowers in a tree, these minor figures are leaves, twigs and branches. A flower's true beauty can be enjoyed only with leaves, twigs and branches. W. Harding remarks: "Unfortunately, as is the case so often in literary search, there continues to be an over-emphasis on the major figures with studies being done and redone *ad nauseum* while the minor figures, who have their own importance of a particular type, are thoroughly neglected. The year 1963 was an exception. Thirty-five books and articles appeared on Emerson and forty-seven on Thoreau. Yet for all the remaining members of the movement there were only ten."[2] Roger C. Mueller expresses a similar opinion: "Numerous articles have since appeared on the relationship of Emerson and Thoreau to the Orient, but very little is known about the later Transcendentalists and their attitudes toward the Orient."[3]

The writers, whom we call minor figures, are really indispensable for understanding any literary movement. It is their presence that helps us to assess the major writers, and, besides, they function as background to the great writers. They may be shadowy figures compared with the broad effulgence of the major writers but they have a role to play in a system. T.S. Eliot's perspective observation on the need of the minor figures out to be mentioned in this context. Eliot writes: "The continuity of a literature is essential to its greatness: it is very largely the function of secondary writers to preserve this continuity, and to provide a body of writing which is not necessarily ready by posterity, but which plays a great part in forming the link between those writers who continue to be read."[4]

In dealing with the minor Transcendentalists I will follow a slightly different method from the one I have followed in the case of Emerson and Thoreau. In dealing with Emerson and Thoreau I discussed a large number of concepts used by both writers which were similar to various philosophical, mystical and ethical concepts of Hinduism. Sometimes, as I have suggested, these concepts were consciously borrowed from Hinduism and sometimes they were mere parallels. The minor Transcendentalists have borrowed very few concepts from Indian sources, nor do we discern a great deal of parallelism between their works and Indian scriptures. As none of them was a serious thinker or writer of eminence, and none of them, - except perhaps Alcott, Clark and Johnson - had read Hindu scriptures extensively, it would be wrong to expect from them any systematically conceptualized thinking. Their contribution to the Transcendental movement, however, lies in their keen interest in Orientalism in general and Hinduism in particular expressed in their lectures and conversations. This general interest enabled them to read and lecture, and sometimes also write on Hindu scriptures and modify their way of life (as, far instance, Alcot did) according to the ideals. Their study of Hindu scriptures through the writings of Sir William Jones and other Oriental scholars opened up new vistas of knowledge for them. They realized that Christianity was not the only path for human salvation. Their encounter with Hinduism also enabled them to see the inherent dogmatism of Christianity. Most of the Transcendentalist were, at one time or the other, members of the Unitarian Church and the next obvious step for them was to accept Transcendentalism whose very basis was hindu idealism. Even the Transcendentalists, like Alcott and Brownson who had no Unitarian background before coming to

Transcendentalism, had passed through brief Unitarian phases. Their interest in Orientalism had another curious effect. The minor Transcendentalists, who could not disocciate themselves completely from the Church, underwent a transformation which enabled them to look at Christianity from a modified point of view. There were still others who endeavoured to interpret Christianity in a new and defensive way to withstand the implicit opposition of Hindu idealism. These minor Transcendentalists who were mostly sympathisers of Emerson and Thoreau helped in creating a climate of opinion in Concord for the growth of Transcendentalism.

Next to Emerson and Thoreau, Amos Bronson Alcott was the most important figure in the Transcendental movement. He was a teacher and a visionary who dreamt of doing many pioneering works to consolidate Transcendentalism and bring about unity of diverse religions. In his young days, he worked as a Yankee peddler in Virginia, a job which gave him an opportunity for self-education and learning of grand manners. He then worked as a teacher in a small Connecticut school where he tried to abolish physical punishment for children. From 1831 to 1834, he taught in a school in Pennsylvania; in 1834 he established the Temple School; in 1859 he became the superintendent of Concord Public Schools, and in 1879 the Dean of the Concord School of Philosophy. Early in life he was interested in the Quaker concept of "inner light" which is closer to the Hindu concept of the in-dwelling spirit in every man, the *Ātman* or the *Brahman*. John T. Reid remarks: "As a young man ... in Philadelphia he became acquainted with Quakers and their doctrine of the 'inner light', which he was to identify with 'Brahma'. About 1831, he taught school for a while in Philadelphia and apparently began to read widely in the well-stocked libraries of the city. It is possible that this reading included some exploration of Indian thought."[5]

Alcott's reading was rather desultory. His chief interest was to unify religions, and he began preparing a list of representative scriptures from all religions to read them. In August 1849, he made a list of books which he designated as Mankind Library. The list included Moses, Confucious, Zoroaster, Pythagoras, Socrates, Plato, Christ, Mahomet, Behmen, Swedenborg. His list of mythology included Hebrew and Egyptian, *Oriental and Indian,* Greek and Roman, Christian and Cosmic. (Italics mine.)[6]

Though this ambitious plan could not be materialised, it indicated the direction in which his mind was moving. Later he made another specific list of Oriental scriptures to be traced at the Athenaeum. The list consisted of Coller's Four Books of Confucious, History of China, (by the Jesuit), The King of Confucious, *The Vedas, The Sama Vedas, Vishnu Purana,* Saadi, Firdusi, The Zendavesta, and The Koran.[7] (Italics mine.)

The most important Hindu scripture, *The Bhagavad Gitā,* which impressed both Emerson and Thoreau influenced Alcott also. He read the *Bhagavad Gitā* sometime in 1846, during which year he also read the writings of Carlyle, Coleridge, Goethe, Swedenborg, and Behmen who were all idealists and mystics. On May 3, 1846, he made an entry in his journals: "In the evening I had an hour's quiet reading of the Oriental wisdom in the Chapters of the *Bhagavat Geeta,* on 'Works' and the 'Performing of Works.'"[8]

This was perhaps Alcott's first reading of any book on Hinduism. This was followed by many other entries in the journal and extracts from the *Bhagavad Gitā* itself. We do not know the source from which he got a copy of the *Bhagavad Gitā*, but as he read the *Gitā* after meeting Emerson, it can be presumed that he might have borrowed the book from Emerson. On May 6, 1846 he wrote in his journals: "I read a lecture in the *Bhagavat Geeta* on 'The Principles of nature and the Vital Spirit.' The whole of this lecture I would transcribe, if I had the time, into my Journal. Have a strong desire to copy the whole of Book XVIII entire - 135 Quarto pages."[9]

On May 8, 1846 he talked to Emerson about the *Bhagavad Gitā*, and about printing the "Bible of Mankind."[10] On May 10, 17 and 19, the same year, he wrote in his journals: "I read more of the *Bhagavat Geeta* and felt how surpassingly fine were the sentiments. These, or selections from the book, should be included in a Bible for Mankind. I think them superior to any of the other Oriental scriptures, the best of all reading for wise men.

Best of books--containing a wisdom blander and far more sane than that of the Hebrews, whether in the mind of Moses or of Him of Nazareth. Were I a preacher, I would venture sometimes to take from its texts the mottos and moral of my discourse. It would be healthful and invigorating to breathe some of this mountain air into the lungs of Christendom."[11]

"This morning ... see Thoreau again. He lends me from the Cholmondeley Collection *The Bhagavad Gitā*, or a Discourse between Krishna and Arjuna on Divine Matters, a Sanskrit Philosophical Poem, Translated, with copious notes, an Introduction on Sanskrit Philosophy, and other matter, by J. Cockburn Thomson, Hartford, England, 1855."[12]

"Arranged the interior of the house for summer. Removed the stove from my study, and disposed pictures and furniture more to my convenience and taste.

Intended to read a little in *Bhagavad Geeta*, but various little chores used up all my day.

Evening: I saw Emerson and had full discourse, mostly on the *Geeta* and the genius of the Oriental faith. I know of no literature more purely intellectual. Its philosophy and poesy seem to me superior too, if not transcending greatly, all others."[13]

The above entries unmistakbly show the extent to which the *Bhagavad Gitā* influenced Alcott. Not only alcott read and understood the *Bhagavad Gitā* but also discussed the spiritual issues involved in it with a sympathetic audience. In June 27, 1849 he made a reference to this: "I dine and pass the afternoon with the Adams and read *Bhagavad Gitā* to a large audience in the evening, with lively discussions etc."[14] One of his interests in the *Bhagavad Gitā* was *Gitā's* emphasis on *Sātwik* food and vegetarianism. Alcott, as we know, was a strict vegetarian for which his friends laughed at him. In the *Tablets*, he quoted from the *Bhagavad Gitā* a verse where the problem of food was discussed: "'All living things,' says the Bhagavad Gita, 'are generated from the bread they eat; bread is generated from rain, rain from divine worship and divine worship from good works.'"[15] Like Thoreau, he was a staunch vegetarian and abstained himself from eating even milk and eggs, and, like orthodox Hindus, exluded certain vegetables from his food, vegetables like potatoes, carrots and beats which grow under the soil, away from sunlight.

This strict vegetarianism led Alcott to establish a Utopian community called Fruitlands. After his visit to England in 1842 where he was enthusiastically greeted by his admirers, he established in Harvard, Massachusetts, his long cherished dream of a spiritual community where, among other things, vegetarianism was to become the prime goal. He purchased a 90 - acre farmland in June 1843, and established the cherished community. Unfortunately, it attracted very few people and most of those who joined it were members of the Alcott family. Due to lack of cooperation and enthusiasm, the project, like other ambitious projects of Alcott's, ended in failure.

The other aspect of the *Bhagavad Gitā* that might have influenced Alcott is its concept of immortality of the soul described in the following verse of the *Gitā*:

> "The Atman is neither born nor does It die. Coming into being and ceasing to be do not take place in It. Unborn, eternal, constant and ancient, It is not killed when the body is slain."[16]

In *Orphic Sayings* Alcott talks about immortality and divinity of the soul more or less in the same vein:

> The grander my conception of being, the nobler my future. There can be no sublimity of life without faith in the soul's eternity. Let me live superior to sense and custom, vigilant always, and I shall experience my divinity; my hope will be infinite, nor shall the universe contain, or content me. But if I creep daily from the haunts of an ignoble past, like a beast from his burrow, neither

> earth nor sky, man nor God, shall appear desirable or glorious; my life shall be loathsome to me, my future reflect my fears. He alone, who lives nobly, oversees his own being, believes all things, and partakes of the eternity of God.[17]

Alcott's another significant achievement was his role in the publication of Sir Edwin Arnold's famous book *The Light of Asia*. Meria Channing, the daughter of W.H. Channing who married Sir Edwin Arnold, brought Buddhism closer to the Transcendentalists. Alcott was instrumental in the publication of Edwin Arnold's book in America. He made several entries in his *Journals* concerning the book. One important entry was: " ... Arnold's *Light of Asia* is already in Press and to be published forthwith. An appendix is to be added to Channing's account of the author, Ripley's and Sanborn's notices, and that of the London Athanaeum. Thus the book will come before our American public chiefly on its own merits. (Holmes also writes a review)."[18] He wrote in another context: "Mr. Niles gives me the English copy of Arnold's *Light of Asia* in exchange for the copy sent me by Mr. Channing which the printers defaced in printing the American edition, now nearly ready for publication. Dr. Holmes' characteristic review, George Ripley's and Channing's letter to me, are published as a supplement.

The book will be read with surprise by most and raise curious questions in the minds of Christians generally."[19]

The book was published in Boston in January, 1880, and subsequently it had 80 edition in America in addition to 60 in England.

Its impact on the American reading public was immense, and it aroused the ire and animosity of many Christian priests who could not tolerate Buddha's doctrine. Alcott fulfilled his role as a propagandist of Orientalism by helping to bring Buddhism to America.

I have said earlier that Alcott was a teacher and a promulgator of mystic ideas from Hinduism as well as from other Eastern sources. In order to fulfill his role as an educator, he established, in 1843, the famous Temple School in Boston. He along with Elizabeth Peabody enrolled 30 boys and girls in the school. The school was a prototype of Montessory school and had many innovative practices both in its organisation and curriculum. They decorated the classrooms with the photographs of Shakespeare, Socrates and Plato. In such beautiful settings Alcott and his fellow teachers conducted classes and held discussions mostly on spiritual matters. The students were allowed to grow freely without much external control and imposition. Alcott himself held a series of conversations with students. His method, unfortunately, was not appreciated by narrow minded clergymen and there was a public uproar when his book- record of conversation on the gospels (2 volumes 1836-1837) appeared. P.F. Boller Jr., says: "Not only did Boston clergymen consider Alcott a 'Theological interloper' for discussing religion (and transcendentally at that) in the class-room; they were also shocked by one particular passage appearing in the appendix: 'And a mother suffers when she had a child. When she is going to have a child she gives up her body to God and He works upon it in a mysterious way and, with her aid, brings forth the child's spirit in a little Body of its own; and when it has come she is blissful.'"[20]

The newspapers like *Daily* Advertiser, *Christian Register, Western Messenger, Quarterly Review* attached Alcott's practice vehemently resulting in a swift decline of enrolment of students in the school. Alcott had to sell the furniture and assets of the school and shift it to his own house in Boston. After some time, when Alcott, true to his belief in human brotherhood, enrolled a blak girl all hell broke loose. Parents quickly withdrew their children, and none but Alcott's three daughters were left. Thus ended Alcott's ambitious educational project. It was difficult for an idealist like Alcott to operate in a world which little understood him. Christy appropriately observes: "Alcott nevertheless appears as something of a Don Quixote in them, an idealist in conflict with a cross world, and 'Lamb among men.'"[21] Although Alcott's ventures such as Mankind Library, Fruitland community and the Temple School ultimately failed, Alcott nevertheless achieved his role as a teacher and a populariser of Orientalism. After Emerson and Thoreau, it was Alcott who read and understood the Indian scriptures and carried their message to America.

Next to Alcott, in order of importance, is James Freeman Clarke (1810-1888), who is regarded, alongwith Samuel Johnson, and a few others like Samuel Longfellow, Thomas Wentworth Higginson and O.B. Frothingham, as belonging to the second generation of the Transcendentalists. J.F. Clarke was the step-grandson of James Freeman, the famous Unitarian. James Freeman was also second in importance to Dr. Channing. Clarke's school education included a training in liberal Christianity. He was responsible for the establishment of Church of the Disciples in Boston in 1841. He was a lifelong friend of Emerson's. Though unlike Emerson and Thoreau, he never bade farewell to Christianity he was considerably influenced by Hinduism. He was a prolific writer and contributed numerous articles to the Unitarian and Transcendental periodicals. The list of the books he read was very impressive, containing more books than Alcott's list. He borrowed these books from the Harvard College Library and the library of the Boston Athenaeum. The list included *Sama Veda*, Stevenson; *Veds*, Rom. Ray: Upham's *Buddhism;* Wilson's *Vishnu Purana; Asiatic Researches*, 1,7; *Rig-Veda* (Samhita); *History of Ancient Sanskrit literature; Indian Epic Poetry*, Williams; Wheeler. *History of India*, 2; Burnouf. *Essais Sur le Veda; Life in Ancient India;* Cox. *Mythology of the Aryan Nations* 1,2.[22] From this one can imagine Clarke's Oriental background. He was a fine scholar and during his long writing career he produced a large number of books such as *Ten Great Religions; Christian Doctrine of Prayer; The Hour which Cometh; Orthodoxy: Its Truths and Errors; Steps of Belief; Self-Culture*. Of these, *Ten Great Religions* was his masterpiece and the most important American book of the 19th Century on Orientalism. It contained a comprehensive chapter on Hinduism and Buddhism, which was later included in the Reverend Edward Hale's revised edition of *The Age of Fable* (1881) by Thomas Bulfinch. The popularity of the book can be assessed from its 22 subsequent editions. Forthingham writes: "All his books, but particularly the 'Ten Great Religions,' show the power of the transcendental idea to render justice to all forms of faith, and give positive interpretations to doctrines obscure and revolting. It detects the truth in things erroneous, the good in things evil."[23] Though Clarke had no formal training in Orientalism like some of his other American Transcendentalists, he could assimilate the complexities of Eastern religions and put them across in a lucid style. His taxonomic division of religions was very much like a classification of a scientist. His analysis of religions was marked by objectivity. For instance, he found Brahminism (his term for Hinduism) lopsided for putting emphasis on spirit and neglecting matter. In Buddhism, he found recognition of man, not God. His love for Buddhism was expressed in his comparison of Buddhism with Protestiantantism. According to him, Buddhism was a revolt against excessive Vedic ritualism, ecclesiasticism and supremacy of Brahmins. He called Buddhism the Protestantism of the East. It might be noted here that all his appreciation and love for Oriental religions did not affect his love for Christianity. He found Christianity superior to Hinduism and other Oriental religions in certain respects, but at the same time appreciated some of the tenets of Eastern religions. Carl T. Jackson says that in Clarke's opinion: "...Christianity had all the positive elements of the Oriental religions, and none of their limitations; it offered a 'ploroma' or fulfillment of all the other religions. Clarke differed from earlier Christian writers only in advocating Christianity as an 'inclusive' rather than an 'exclusive' system. Thus, a place was made for the Oriental religions."[24]

Samuel Johnson (1822-1882), worked on comparative religion somewhat in the manner of Clarke. In fact, both should be studied together because they had quarrelled with each other on many fundamental issues and published their controversies in the *Radical*. As a Transcendentalist, Johnson was an individualist like Thoreau. Frothingham says: "While Mr. Channing trusted in social combinations, and Mr. Clarke put his faith in organized religion, he had a clear eye to the integrity of the separate soul. He attended no conventions, joined no societies, worked with no associations, had confidence in no parties, sects, schemes, or combinations, but nursed his solitary thought, delivered his personal message, bore his private witness, and there rested."[25] Johnson, like many other Transcendentalists, started as a Unitarian but unlike Clarke he resigned from the Unitarian ministry after only one year and started preaching in a non-denominational Church. Like some of his fellow Transcendentalists he was an enthusiastic social reformer and demonstrated his interest in concepts like liberty and progress. He was also interested, like Clarke and others, in the religions of the East and the results of his interest and research culminated in the publication of *Oriental Religions and Their Relation to Universal Religion, India* (1873). This book is Johnson's remarkable achievement and "none save a Transcendentalist could have succeeded in extracting so much deep spiritual meaning from the symbols and practices of those ancient faiths."[26] Before writing the book, Johnson and Clarke, as mentioned above, engaged in polemics in the pages of *The Radical,* the point of the quarrel being the relation of Christianity to other religions, particularly Hinduism. His point of view was that the sacred books of the world are only "threads on which (the religions) have strung their own inspirations, imaginations and desires ... Not the thread, but that which was hung upon it, was after all the substance of belief."[27] Though Clarke himself was a comparative religionist he had not forsaken Christianity and Johnson's charge about the fallibility of the Bible was difficult for him to swallow. Clarke replied to Johnson in a rejoinder: "The radical certainly considers Christ and the Bible as a source of Truth -- only he does not go to them so much as to others. He goes to science; he goes to the Vedas, (when he can find them); he goes to Emerson and Thoreau; he goes to Theodore Parker, Harbert Spencer and Miss Cobbe."[28] Johnson answered Clarke's charge in an article entitled "James Freeman Clarke on Authority."[29] He opposed Clarke because Clarke "does not find God represented as the Universal Father and all men as brothers anywhere in the Ethnic Religions, and thinks we may infer from this that 'Christ is the one Mediator of these truths.'"[30] Johnson further remarked: "Let me say in general, what I hope one day to prove more fully, that I find all through the Oriental Religions vigorous germs of these great natural beliefs, quite adequate to guarantee their fullest expansion in Christianity."[31] In another article he discusses the same point once again with greater conviction and vigour: "We dream we have sight of special moral truth never known before, and celebrate our Christian prerogatives therein. Then some scholar pores over an old Bhagavatgitā or Zendavasta of the Gentiles, or older Vedic psalmody of what to us is the Morning of time, and brings forth thence the treasures of aspiration and recognition that are the guarantees of our best. Some didactic Confucius is seen in far antiquity drawing purest moral doctrine from the wells of a Past that seemed remote even to him; or some brave democratic Buddha protesting against the tyranny of caste in the name of a 'Law of grace for all'. Surely it is an ungracious and unbecoming task to strive as many do, over (z)ealous for that honour to Jesus and the Bible ... to disparge these evidence".[32]

His views on Oriental religions were consolidated in his book *Oriental Religion*. The book was a result of his incessant labour for more than 20 years after he retired from the non-denomentional church in 1870. The first volume on India was published in 1872, the second volume on China in 1877, and the last volume on Persia in 1882. In the volume on India he has discussed comprehensively many Indian scriptures. His discussion of *Ṛg Veda*, for example, cover 65 pages. *The Laws of Manu* covers 32 pages and *Vedānta* covers 69 pages. The passages, he quotes from *Ṛg Veda* concerning transcendental wisdom, may be quoted here to demonstrate Johnson's wisdom in selecting and understanding them:

> That which is beyond the earth and sky, beyond gods and spirits; what earliest embryo did the waters hold, in which all the gods were assembled? Ye know not Him who produced these things. Something else is within you. The chanters of hymns go about enveloped in mist, and unsatisfied with idle talk.[33]
>
> Who has seen the First Born? Where was the life, the blood, the soul of the world? Who went to ask it of any that knew it.[34]
>
> What the tree from which they shaped heaven and earth? Wise men, ask indeed, in your minds, on what He stood when He held the worlds.[35]
>
> It is the inadequacy of all conceptions of Original Cause as a definite form of existence that one of these poets would express when he says, "The existent sprang from that which exists not."[36]

Johnson, as a Transcendentalist, understood the purport of *Advaita Vedāntin* properly. Like a Vedantin he refused to accept the distinction between the so-called sacred and the profane, good and bad, divine and human. The key phrase in his discussion of Hindu philosophy is "infinite mind" which is akin to Brahman and Emerson's Over-Soul. As a comparative religionist he had a very perceptive mind. He could see similarities between the Christian gospel and the Hindu laws, especially those codified by Manu. The following passage describes the nature of his orientalism:

> "God is Spirit" says the Christian Gospel, "and they who worship Him must worship Him in Spirit and in Truth." Here the Hindu Law:- "O friend to virtue, that Supreme Spirit, which thou believest one with thy-self, resides in thy bosom perpetually, and is an all knowing inspector of thy virtue or thy crime."
>
> (*Manu, VIII, 91.*)
>
> "If thou art not at variance with that great divinity within thee, go not on pilgrimage to Ganga, nor to the plain of Curu." (*Ibid.92.*)
>
> "The soul is its own witness, its own refuge. Offend not thy conscious soul, the supreme internal witness of men." "The wicked have said in their hearts, "None sees us." Yes, the gods see them, and the spirit within their own breasts." (*Manu VIII, 84,85.*)
>
> "The wages of sin," says the Christian Bible, "is death." Quite as distinctly says the Hindu Law:-
>
> "In whatever extremity, never turn to sin." (*Manu IV, 171.*)
>
> "Vice is more dreadful by reason of its penalties than death." (*Manu VII, 53.*)

"Whosoever" says the New Testament, "shall break one of these commandments, is guilty of all." The Dharmasastra of Manu affirms the same natural law of integrity. "If one sins with one member, the sin destroys his virtue, as a single hole will let out all the water in flask." (*Manu II, 99.*)

"... The only firm friend who follows man after death is justice."

(*Manu VIII, 17.*)[37]

Johnson also criticised Hinduism for its "mystical dreaminess and antimaterial qualities." His obsession with "transcendental evolutionism" prevented him from looking properly into Hinduism. Though he had a broad universal attitude of mind which is a *sine qua non* of a comparative religionist, his "transcendental evolutionism" and "priorism" sometimes blur the focus of his discussion. In the words of Carl T. Jackson: "The major weakness of Johnson's work was its a *priorism*: all data were pressed into support of his transcendental evolutionism. His formulations, like Clarke's were frequently gross oversimplifications. Thus, he characterized the Hindu mind as cerebral and introspective, the Chinese mind as muscular and plodding, and the Persian mind as nervous and mediating. The problems created by such a classification can be seen in the difficulty with which he explained how Buddhism, a product of Indian cerebrality, could have rooted itself in a muscular China. Taoism, he had to claim, was not so mystical as had been believed, but merely another expression of Chinese practicality and concreteness. The immensity of the three volumes, a certain heaviness in style, and an indulgence in frequent anti-Christian barbs Prevented

Johnson's work from ever enjoying the wide popularity gained by Clarke's book. Nevertheless, his discussion was frequently referred to in writings of the period."[38]

Despite his criticism of Hinduism, his study of Indian scriptures and religion was based upon his admiration and love for the Orient, an admiration which he shared with Emerson and Thoreau.

William Henry Channing (1810-1884) was related to Dr. W.E. Channing (1780-1842) who was a chief spokesman for the New England Unitarianism and was called a transcendentalist before the advent of Transcendentalism. W.H. Channing was a vigorous Transcendentalist. He was connected with the journal, *The Western Messanger*, and for a whole year was its sole editor. He was associated with the group of Transcendentalists who accepted Brownson, not Emerson, as the leader. His connection in Indian scriptures is chiefly seen in *The Spirit of the Age,* which was reprinted in the *Dial*. It contained generous extracts from the *Bhagavad Gitā*. In fact, for the first time, passages from the *Bhagavat Gitā* appeared in *The Dial*. Out of 18 chapters of the *Bhagavad Gitā,* eight important ones were selected, and long extracts were taken from these. These contained summaries of the philosophy of *Sānkhya* and *Yoga* and the concept of *Purusa, Prakruti* and *Brahman*. In *The Spirit of the Age* some sections from *Hitopadesa* of Veeshnoo Sarma were published. Emerson had earlier published the moral teachings of *Hitopadesa* excluding the story element. Towards the latter part of his life, in 1880, Channing delivered four lectures[39] relating to Orientalism to a gathering in Concord. The titles of the lectures were: "Historical Mysticism"; "Man's Fourfold Being"; "True Buddhism"; and "Modern Pessimism."

Among the members of the Transcendental Club Orestes Augustus Brownson (1803-1876), was an important and active member. In a sense, he was regarded as a representative figure in Transcendentalism. In his early life he was influenced by Calvinism which developed in him a sense of morbidity. The following passage clearly indicates the extent of the influence of Calvinism on him: "Now ends another year. Yes, I have sinned everyday, every hour, year, and every breath has been drawn in iniquity: every thought and every imagination of my heart has been evil, only evil, and that continually ... How little do I feel religion, how cold, how dead in the service of the Lord: -- I see nothing in me that looks like religion; I am base; I am corrupt, -- lost to every sense of religion."[40] He was so disenchanted with Calvinism that he was eager to accept any other doctrine that opposed its grim pessimism. It was the Church of Universalism that immediately attracted him. In 1826, he applied to the Universalist General Convention for a job as a preacher. On June 26 of the same year he was ordained as a preacher. He continued as a preacher for sometime, but gradually became sceptical of Christian doctrines. He rejected the idea that Christian scriptures were the revealed words of God. He also started questioning the very existence of God. In 1831, he switched his allegiance to Unitarianism. Though he formally declared that he was an independent preacher, belonging to no Christian denomination, he said in the same breath that his religious views were closer to Unitarianism. He wrote in *The Philanthropist:* "Should I assume the name of any party, it should be Unitarian, as that denomination approximates near, in my estimation, to the Spirit of Christianity than any other. Unitarian discourses are mostly Practical; their lessons inculcate charity, a refined moral feeling and universal benevolence.... but I discover no necessity of assuming any name that can become the rellying point of a sect ..... I am an independent preacher, accountable to my God to truth, to my country, to the people of my Church, but to no other tribunal."[41]

In 1832, he actually became a Unitarian priest and in 1836 published his first imxortant book *New Views of Christianity, Society and the Church*. During this phase he became interested in Transcendentalism like other Unitarian ministers, and showed a great deal of interest in the Indian lore. Like Emerson he believed that Western idealism was borrowed or influenced by the idealism of the *Upaniṣads*. He thus writes in *New Views:*

> At the very moment when the sigh had just escaped, that mystic land reappeared. The English, through the East India Company, had brought to light its old literature and philosophy, so diverse from the literature and philosophy of the modern Europe or of a Classical antiquity, and men were captivated by their novelty and bewildered by their strangeness. Sir William Jones gave currency to them by his poetical paraphrases and limitations; and the Asiatic Society by its researches placed them within reach of the learned of Europe. The Church rejoiced, for it was like bringing back her long lost mother, whose features she had remembered and was able at once to recognize. Germany, England, and even France became oriental, Cicero, and Horace, and Virgil, Aeschylus, Euripedes, and even Homer, with Jupiter, Apollo, and Minerva were forced to bow before Hindoo bards and gods of uncouth forms and unutterable names.

> The influence of the old Brahminical or spiritual world, thus dug up from the grave of centuries, may be traced in all our philosophy, art and literature. It is remarkable in our poets. It moulds the form in Byron, Penetrates to the ground in Wordsworth and entirely predominates in the Schlegels. It causes us to feel a new interest in those writers and those epochs which partake the most of spiritualism. Those old English writers who were somewhat inclined to mysticism are revived; Plato, who travelled in the East and brought back its lore which he modified by Western genius and moulded into Grecian forms, is re-edited, commented on, translated, and raised to the highest rank among philosophers.[42]

That Brownson was influenced by the Hindu lore can be demonstrated in his use of the Hindu concept of ten *avatārs* of God: "Our Protestant populations, on whom the sun of the reformation shines in its effulgence, are moved, run towards their teaching, and are about to hail it as the Tenth Avatar come to redeem the world."[43] Though Brownson was a spiritual drifter, he was convinced that Indian scriptures, embodying the ideals of Hinduism, have a pervasive influence in shaping his mind and vision and giving him the flexibility necessary for developing a holistic approach to religions.

George Ripley (1802-1880), who was a close friend of Brownson, was "one of the noblest and most appealing Americans of his time." Before Transcendentalism became a systematic doctrine, he wrote numerous essays in *The Christian Examiner* criticising materialism, which later became the basis of the Transcendentalism. Later in 1838 he started publishing in Boston a valuable Transcendental project named *Specimens of Foreign Standard Literature*. He also helped Margaret Fuller to publish the Transcendental journal *The Dial* founded in 1840. He was a literary critic for the *New York Tribune* and became one of the founder members of *Harper's New Monthly Magazine* (1850). He was an ardent Unitarian preacher and continued in the same job till 1841. The same year, with a small band of friends and followers comprising teachers, preachers, musicologists, writers and aristocratic ladies, he started Brook Farm, and Utopian Community experience based on Transcendental idealism whose motto was simple living and high thinking. He and his wife Sophia, an intelligent and sensitive woman, dedicated their life for that cause. They "quite literally gave their blood, sweat, and tears to the enterprise." In the words of Charles Crowe, "He (Repley) had thought of Brook Farm as an experimental reform centre for the nation, destiny of the nation, perhaps of the whole world."[44] It is interesting to note that Emerson refused to join the Brook Farm experiment and preferred to remain as a meditative philosopher in his small house in Concord. A committee consisting of Ripley, Fuller and Alcott Ripley's wife visited Emerson in 1840 and requested him to join the project. Emerson was not willing to leave his home and curtly replied: "I do not wish to move from my present prison to a prison a little larger." He wrote in a letter: "I have decided not to join it and yet very slowly and I may almost say penitentially ... The ground of my decision is almost purely personal to myself ... the community is not good for me .... If the community is not good for me neither am I good for it."[45] The Brook Farm experiment, as we know, ended tragically in 1847 after a big fire destroyed the main building.

Like his fellow Transcendentalists, Ripley had considerable interest in the literature and philosophy of India. His review of Edwin Arnold's *Light of Asia* shows his love of Buddhism. He writes in the review: "As an exposition of the religious system of Buddha we reckon this poem as no more successful than the numerous similar attempts in prose. We have no sufficient data for the solution of the problem. But as a magnificent work of imagination and a sublime appeal in the interests of the loftiest human virtue, we tender it the sincerest welcome, and grasp the author by the hand as a genuine prophet of the soul."[46]

Theodore Parker (1810-1860), was an important figure among the historians of American ideas. He was known in the Transcendental circle for his erudition, his powerful preaching, and his moral reform movement. He was a prodigious scholar who mastered not less than 20 different languages. His interest in the Orient specifically India can be judged from the books he borrowed from the Harvard College Library: *Sir Wm. Jones's Works: Dubois India; Rhode-Hindus; Jones on the Canon* etc.[47] In Boston, he came in contact with two important leaders of the New England renaissance, Dr. William Ellery Channing and Emerson, and through this contact he got interested in Transcendentalism. Unlike J.F. Clarke who started with Judaism, Parker started with Brahmanism. In Clarke's book *Ten Great Religions* Judaism was the Centre, whereas in Parker it was Brahminism. He asked a very significant question, "What was the discovery of America, the English Revolution, the American, the French? Nay, what were these six great historic forms of religion-Brahminic, Hebraistic, Classic, Buddhistic, Christian, Mahommedan-they would be what February and March are to May, July, September and October...?"[48]

Parker was known for his anti-Christian doctrines which sparked off controversy among the believers. He denounced certain Christian practices in very strong terms. Transcendentalism and Hinduism undoubtedly influenced him in his anti-Christian stance.

Jones Very (1813-1880) was another minor Transcendentalist and a mystic poet whose self-effacing, esoteric and mystical poetry had some strain of the Orient. He was better known as a minor 19th century poet and scholar than a Transcendentalist. As a poet, he had some strokes of madness which could be compared with the madness of the Romantic poets. Quite early in his life he showed mystical traits and it was said that he received spiritual communication from the Holy Ghost and had mystical visions. Emerson encouraged him. In 1843, he became a Unitarian preacher but preached very little. Whenever he preached he had divine inspiration. He claimed that his religious poems were dictated by the Holy Ghost himself. A reviewer of his poems and essays wrote in *The Dial*, July 11, 1841: "These sonnets have little range of topics, no extent of observation, no playfulness there is even a certain torpidity in the concluding lines of some of them, which reminds one of church hymns; but, whilst they flow with great sweetness, they have the sublime unity of the Decalogue or the Code of Menu, and if as monotonous, yet are they almost as pure as the sounds of surrounding Nature."[49]

He had considerable influence on other Transcendentalists. William Irving Bartlett writes: "His brilliant but disturbing personality made so stunning an impact on Emerson, Nathaniel Hawthorne, M. Fuller, Alcott, W.R. Channing and the Peabody sisters, has never before been adequately understood by students of American Transcendentalism."[50]

Critics, including Arthur Christy, have not done full justice to Very's Orientalism. His pure life, his complete reliance on God and his mystic communion with Him resembled him to an Indian mystic. His views on self-reliance have resemblance to Emerson's self-reliance, doctrine of compensation, and Over-Soul.

Moncure Conway (1823-1907), was another minor Transcendentalist who had true love for India and her religions. The religions of India so much influenced him that he made a pilgrimage to India and on his return recounted his experience in his spiritual travelogue *My Pilgrimage to the Wise Men of the East*. His interest in the Orient was aroused quite early. It was Emerson who advised him and lent him a book on Persia and India, and introduced him to Wilkins translation of the *Bhagavad Gitā*. For Conway, "The sun of civilization rose in the East and ever Journey Westward."[51] Again, he wrote in his travelogue: "It was in studying the Oriental books in my youth that I learned that in all the earth were growing the flowers and fruits of the human heart, concerning which one wise Man said, 'Keep thy heart above all that thou guardest; for out of it are the issues of life'."[52] During his visit to New Delhi he reminisced: "In my youth Emerson loaned me the Bhagavad Gita (Wilkin's translation), and my interest in original thought began with the dialogue between Arjuna and Krishna. Later I found the whole story of the Mahabharata finally told by my friend Mrs. Manning in her "Ancient and Mediaeval India." Even forty years ago one has to search out what is now accessible to all. It was thrilling to find myself at the Pillared gateway of the fortified city, traditionally supposed to be the capital of the Pandavas during their long struggle with the Kuravas."[53]

He decried the works of the Christian missionaries who always distorted the image of India: "At every movement in India I had to lament the narrowness of our English and American theologians and professors who, in their gratuitous jealousy for the originality of everything in the Bible, implanted even in the most liberal of us their pupils a notion that there was at end before the beginning of our era a great gulf fixed between the Holy Land and India, so that nothing could have been possibly derived thereform by Christianity. That error is now exploded, even in Protestant countries, - for the Greek and Roman churches must be credited with having for the most part ignored this error.[54]

Frederic Henry Hedge (1805-1890), another minor figure in the Transcendentalist group, was a distinguished teacher at Harvard and got interested in Indian scriptures when he was a Professor of Ecclesiastical History at the Harvard Divinity School from 1857 to 1876. The books he borrowed from Harvard College library indicated his acquaintance with Hinduism and Indian literature. The books were: Maurice's *Indian Antiquities* vols. 1 to 7; Sir Wm. Jone's 'Works' vols. 3,4 and 9; *Asiatic Researches* vols. 3 and 8; and Williams' *Sakuntala* etc.[55] After visiting Boston, where he met Emerson, he joined the Transcendental Club. His book *Reason in Religion*, published in 1865, was a brilliant argument in defence of a transcendentalized christianity.

Thomas Wentworth Higginson (1823-1911), a very minor Transcendentalist was a moralist and noted for his active participation in antislavery movement. He was interested in India and edited a selection of Max Muller's translation of *Dhammapada* for publication in the *Radical* and called it "The Buddhist 'Path of

Virtue.'" His interest in Buddhism was particularly helpful to the Transcendentalists. Talking about the missionary activities of Ashok for Buddhism Higginson wrote: "More than two thousand years have now passed, and we are opening this tomb again; the lights still burn, the flowers are still fresh, the perfume of the noble life yet remains immortal."[56] At the world Parliament of Religions, held in Chicago in 1893, he delivered a lecture "The Sympathy of Religion" in which he praised Buddhism by quoting *Dhammapada:* "We are all engaged in that magnificent work described in the Buddhist *Dhammapada* or Path of Light: 'make thyself an island; work hard, be wise.' If each could make himself an island, there would yet appear at last above these waves of despair or doubt, a continent fairer than Columbus won."[57]

In the essay called "Water-lilies" published in the *Atlantic* in September 1858, he praised Buddhism. Higginson says the symbol of lily is sacred:

> They are Nature's symbols of coolness. They suggest to us the white garments of their Oriental worshippers ....
>
> Open the Vishnu Purana at any page, and it is a *Sortes Lilianae*. The orb of the earth is Lotus-shaped, and is upborne by the tusks of Vesava, as if he had been sporting in a lake where the leaves and blossoms float. Brahma, first incarnation of Vishnu, creator of the world, was born from a Lotus; so was Sri or Lakshmi, the Hindoo Venus, Goddess of beauty and prosperity, protectress of womanhood, whose worship guards the house from all danger, "Seated on a full-blown

> Lotus, and holding a Lotus in her hand, the goddess Sri, radiant with beauty, rose from the waves."
>
> The mystic formula or "mani" is imprinted on the pavement of the streets, it floats on flags from the temples, and the wealthy Buddhists maintain sculptormissionaries, Old Mortalities of the waterlily, who wandering to distant lands, carve the blessed words upon cliff and stone.
>
> The second of the eighteen Hindoo Puranas is styled the Padma Purana, because it treats of the "epoch when the world was a golden Lotus", and the sacred incantation which goes murmuring through Thibet is "Om mani Padme houm."[58]

Long before, Thoreau wrote in his *Journal* on June 26, 1852:

> "... our Lotus, queen of the waters .... How sweet, innocent, wholesome its fragrance: How pure its white petals, though its root is in the mud! It must answer in my mind for what the Orientals say of the lotus flower."[59]

In one of Higginson's unpublished manuscripts a document entitled "My Creed" is found where his spiritual view is put in a very succinct manner:

> In the life of every thoughtful man, no matter how sunny his temperament, there are moments of care, sorrow, depression, perplexity when neither study nor action nor friends will clear the horizon.

> ....It is at such times that the thought of an unseen Power comes to help him; by no tradition of the Churches, with no apparatus of mythology; but simply in the form that the mystics call 'the flight of the Alone, to the Alone! ... It may be in a church; it may equall; well be in a solitary room or a mountain height .... The test of such an experience, call it prayer or reverie or what you please - is as substantial as anything that can come to us. .. I am not so sure of what I see with my eyes - not so sure that two and two make four - not so sure of any of the forms of the logical syllogism as I am of the genuineness and value of these occasional movements ....[60]

Higginson's broad view of religions his attempts to reconcile various world faiths, his contribution to Transcendentalism, and his love for Buddhism are significant. He can be said to have bridged the gap between the earlier Transcendentalists and their latter-day disciples.

To sum up, the minor Transcendentalists who carried forward the work of Emerson and Thoreau contributed very significantly to the dissemination of ideas of Oriental religions in America and thus took the Eastern religions to the doorstep. Americans of the 19th century Broadly speaking, Emerson and Thoreau were the intellectual idealists, secluded in their own niches of power and prestige, away from the common concerns of ordinary men and women but these minor Transcendentalists, in thier own meaningful way, sprinkled the ideas of world religions among the people and made Transcendentalism a pervasive ideal.

Footnotes:

1. Perry Miller, *The Transcendentalists: An Anthology* (1950; rpt. Massachusetts: Harvard Univ. Press, 1967), Intro. 5.

2. Walter Harding, "Emerson, Thoreau, and Transcendentalism," *American Literary Scholarship* (1963), p.15

3. Roger C. Mueller, "Transcendental Periodicals and the Orient," in *The Minor and Later Transcendentalists: A Symposium*, ed. E. Gittleman (Hartford: Transcendental Books, 1969), p.52.

4. T. S. Eliot, quoted by J.C. Levenson, in "Christopher Pearse Cranch: The Case History of a Minor Artist in America," *American Literature*, 21 (1949-1950), p.415.

5. John T. Reid, p.45.

6. Christy, *The Orient*, p. 241.

7. Ibid. p.243.

8. Alcott, *The Journals of Bronson Alcott*, ed. Odell Shepard (Boston: Little, Brown and Co., 1938), p.178.

9. Ibid., p.179.

10. Ibid. p. 180.

11. Ibid., (May 10,1846)

12. Ibid., p. 282 (May 13, 1856)

13. Ibid., p. 181. (May 17, 1846)

14. See Christy, *The Orient*, p.242.

15. A.B. Alcott, *Tablets* (Boston: Roberts Brothers, 1868), p. 16.

16. *Bhagavad Gitā*, p. 139. (II: 20).

17. Alcott, "Orphic Saying," in *The Transcendentalists: An Anthology*, p.304.

18. Christy, *The Orient*, p.251. (quoted).

19. Ibid.

20. P.F. Boller, *American Transcendentalism*, p.108.

21. *The Orient*, p. 258.

22. K. W. Cameron, *Transcendental Reading Patterns* (Hartford:Transcendental Books, 1970).

23. O. B. Frothingham, *Transcendentalism in New England: A History* (1876; rpt. New York: Harper Touchbooks, 1959), p.344.

24. Carl T. Jackson, p.433.

25. Frothingham, *Transcendentalism*, p.347.

26. Ibid., p.345.

27. Quoted by R.C. Mueller, "Transcendental Periodicals and the Orient," p.54. [*Radical*, I (1865-66) 115].

28. Ibid., [*Radical*, I (1865-66) 150]

29. Ibid., p.55. [*Radical*, I (1865-66) 218-26]

30. Ibid.
31. Ibid.

32. Ibid. [*Radical,* I (1865-66) 239]

33. Samuel Johnson, *Oriental Religions and Their Relation to Universal Religion: India* (Boston: James R. Osgood and Co., 1873), p.119. (*Ṛg.* X:82).

34. Ibid. (*Ṛg.* I:164:4)

35. Ibid. (*Ṛg.* X:81:4)

36. Ibid. (*Ṛg.* X:72:2)

37. Ibid. pp. 182-183.

38. Carl T. Jackson, p. 434.

39. *The Orient,* p. 365.

40. Quoted by Americo D. Lapati, *Orestes A Brownson* (Conn.: Twayne Publishers, Inc., 1965), pp. 24-25.

41. Ibid., p.30 [*The Philanthropist,* II, 86].

42. O.A. Brownson, "New Views," *Works,* ed. H.P. Brownson (Detroit: H.P. Brownson, 1898), IV, pp. 26-27.

43. Ibid., VI, pp.112-113.

44. Charles Crowe, *George Ripley:Transcendentalist and Utopian Socialist* (Athens: Univ. of Georgia Press, 1967), p.175.

45. *Letters,* II, p. 369-370.

46. O.B. Frothingham, *George Ripley* (Boston: Houghton, Mifflin and Co., 1882), pp. 227-228.

47. Cameron, *Transcendental Reading Patterns,* pp.90- 129.

48. Rev. Theodore Parker, "A Sermon," *ESQ*. 59 (Sprint, 1970), p. 89.

49. *The Dial* (July, 1841) II, 130-131.

50. William Irving Bartlett, *Jones Very: Emerson's "Brave Saint"* (New York: Greenwood Press, 1968), p.89.

51. Moncure Daniel Conway, *My Pilgrimage to the Wise Men of the East* (Boston and New York: Houghton, Mifflin and Co., 1906), p. 3.

52. Ibid., p. 2.

53. Ibid., p.282.

54. Ibid., pp. 300-301.

55. Cameron, *Transcendental Reading Patterns*, pp. 171-186.

56. Quoted by R.C. Mueller, p.56. [*Index*, III (1872), 83].

57. Col. T.W.Higginson, "Sympathy of Religion," *The World's Parliament of Religions*, ed. Rev. John Henry Barrows (Chicago: The Parliament Pub. Co., 1893), p.782.

58. Higginson, "Water-lilies," *The Atlantic Monthly*, II, No. XI (September, 1858), pp. 469, 470, 471.

59. *Journal*, VI, pp. 147-148.

60. Mary Thacher Higginson, *Thomas Wentworth Higginson: the Story of his Life* (Boston and New York Houghton Mifflin Co., 1914), pp. 268-269.

VI

CONCLUSION

Our discussion of the American Transcendentalists in previous chapters brings us to a stage where it is necessary to arrange the tangled threads together and make a few generalizations on the basis of our analysis and findings. We may also here re-state our perspective and show in what way the movement was related to the Indian scriptures. Our major premises and hypotheses were that the American Transcendentalist movement in its philosophical and mystical framework was basically influenced by the seminal ideas from Hindu philosophy epitomized in the *Upaniṣads*. To Emerson and Thoreau and, to a certain extent their followers, Asia meant principally India. The influence of other civilizations of Asia such as Chinese, Persian and Arabian on Transcendentalism was superficial and negligible. A clear stream of the Upanisadic idealism and other allied Hindu scriptures flooded the minds of the Transcendentalists and helped them consolidate and crystallize their own line of thinking. The Indian scriptures such as the *Ṛg Veda Samhitā, Sam Veda, the Upaniṣads* (such as *Kaṭha* and *Maṇḍaka*), *The Mahābhārata, Law of Manu, The Bhagavad Gitā,*

Sānkhya Kārika, *Nyāya Sutras*, *Mimamsā*, *The Vishnu Purana*, *The Bhāgavata Purāna*, *The Dhammapada* were some of the scriptures which the Transcendentalists were familiar with. Most of these texts, as we know, were translated into English and published by the Asiatic Society of Bengal and were made available to the 19th century Americans through traders and missionaries. Besides these religious texts, the literary texts which they read included Vishnu Sharma's *Hitopadesa*, Kalidasa's *Megha Duta* and *Sakuntalā*, the Story of Nala and Damayanti, select specimens from the Theatre of the Hindus, India epic poetry and history of Sanskrit literature. Apart from this direct knowledge of Indian scriptures and literary texts, the Transcendentalists also had the quintessence of the Indian concepts filtered through early Greek thinkers like Plato, Pythagoras, Plotinus etc. who, as we know, influenced Transcendentalism in its initial stage.

The American Transcendental movement can be seen as part of a general cultural renaissance which tried to develop a holistic approach to life and religions. This phenomenon brought together various religions of the world and embodied an eclectic and comprehensive vision of the Universe. This cultural renaissance was the result of several links between America and Asia from the Pre-Columbian days to the 19th century. This broad spectrum of cultural continuity between America and Asia helps us to see the mid-nineteenth century phenomenon of Transcendentalism as a transitional phase looking forward to the twentieth century when links between India and America have become deeper and wider. Transcendentalism has had its effect both on the radicals and the conservatives. Writers, philosophers, politicians, clergymen etc. have been fascinated by the variety and splendour that India has offered to them. Archaeologists and historians like De Guignes (following the historian Li Yen of China,) Alexander Von Homboldt, Heine-Geldern and Gordern and Gorden Ekholm, Samuel Marti, A.M. Garibay, Paul Kirchhoff and Dennis Louy have archaeological evidence to prove the early cultural links between India and the American continents, and suggest that the links may continue because of their vestigial character.

During the early days of America, philosophers and clergymen like Cotton Mather, William Adan Jabez, T. Sunderland and Theodore Parker, W.E. Channing, Charles Dall and J.S. Holmes and many others tried to accelerate the process of understanding betwen the two countries by their genuine attempts to know and understand India. The Unitarian priests played a vital role in this. Trade and missionary activities paved the way for intellectual activities. Scholars like Sir William Jones of Calcutta established liaison between the Historical Society of Bengal. Institutions like the Anthology Club and the Historical Society of Massachusettes created strong interests in India. The pioneering work of these scholars and institutions in bringing America and India closer paved the way for fuller understanding of the two cultures. Creative artists in the 19th century took advantage of these explorations and utilized them in their writings. Edgar Allan Poe, Herman Melville, Walt Whitman and John Greenleaf Whittier and many others used Indian myths and symbols in their writings. The influence of India continued throughout nineteenth century and became vigorous in the twentieth. The "new humanists" like Irving Babbitt, Paul Elmore More etc. got the inspiration from the Indian religions and aesthetics. In the 1950s and 60s, such influence was widespread. The "new transcendentalists" and bohemians like Gary Snyder, Allen Ginsberg, Lawrence Ferlinghetti, Thomas Merton etc. benefitted from such influences and created around them a cult whose basis was Indian religions and ways of life. The influence of Indian philosophy and religions on America encouraged idealism and discouraged utilitarianism and hedonism to some extent, broadening the concept of philosophy, metaphysics and psychology.

Emerson and Thoreau were the two important 19th century writers whose contributions to cultural synthesis between America and India were immense. We have shown how Emerson had meticulously read and digested the essence of Hindu idealism and mysticism propounded by the *Upaniṣhads* and the *Bhagavad Gitā*. The main trend in Indian philosophy has always been the pragmatic aspect of human life aiming at attainment of liberation. Emerson, true to this spirit of Indian philosophy, emphasized the practical aspect of life along with the metaphysical. He was perhaps the only 19th century philosopher and creative writer who developed a conceptual system of philosophy based on the Hindu concepts like "Over Soul," law of Karma (law of compensation), fate, immortality of soul etc. In him the best of the East, and the best of the West merge into a unified system. Disparities between religions disappear in his vision of the Universe. The basis of this unification, as we already know, is the Upanishadic concept of life. Later scientists, particularly physicists, have been deeply influenced by such a unified vision and have tried to show in their conception of the universe that Eastern religions and modern physics complement each other, instead of cancelling each other, as is usually believed. Christy's opinion that Emerson "was an endless seeker and experimenter who clung to no definite tradition,"[1] can be challenged in view of the fact that although Emerson dabbled in many Oriental religions, his mind and heart were set on India and there is a stream of Indian thought flowing through all his writings.

Thoreau, like Emerson, derived spiritual inspiration from such Hindu scriptures as the *Bhagavad Gitā*, the *Law of Manu*, etc. Whereas the influence of Hindu scriptures on Emerson was principally on his conceptualized thought, in Thoreau's case it was on a practical level of moulding a life. Thoreau became a practical *yogi* and not an idealist thinker. *A Week* can be seen as a symbolic divine journey in search of meaning in life and the Walden experiment can be viewed in the light of yoga. Stein's study of Thoreau as a *Jnāna yogi* and Mac Shane's study of him as a *Karma yogi* are correct expositions of his Indian connections. Thoreau can also be called a *Raja yogi* in the light of Patanjali's *Astānga yoga*, an idea which I have discussed in Chapter 4. His doctrine of civil disobedience which was appreciated and used by Mahatma Gandhi is another proof of his temperamental and spiritual kinship with India.

Emerson and Thoreau have, to some extent, eclipsed their contemporaries, the minor Transcendentalists by their strong personalities and profound intellectual concerns. It is unfortunate that these minor figures who have in their own way contributed to the stream of thought are neglected by critics, and this neglect has seriously affected our knowledge and understanding of the Transcendental milieu. When major figures were busy in metaphysical speculations, evolving conceptual theories, the minor figures were engaged in organising meetings, establishing schools, founding utopian communes, publicizing transcendental ideals and eradicating social maladies. If Emerson and

Thoreau were the protagonists in a play, the minor figures were accessory to the effectiveness of the play. Hence for a right appraisal of Transcendentalism, one has to take into consideration the roles of the major writers as well as the roles of the minor figures.

To sum up, the mainstream of the Transcendentalist thought and action was rigidly determined by Indian scriptures, the essence of which were Hindu idealism and mysticism. We may say with a great deal of conviction and certainty that the spiritual depth, magnitude and dimention the Transcendentalists have achieved would not have been possible without the influence of Indian scriptures on them.

Footnote:

1. Christy, *The Orient*, p. 263.

SELECT BIBLIOGRAPHY

Primary Sources:

Alcott, A. Bronson. *The Journals*. Ed. Odell Shepard. Boston:Little, Brown & Co., 1938.

Tablets. Boston: Roberts Brothers, 1868.

American Transcendentalists: Their Prose and Poetry. Ed. Perry Miller. New York:Doubleday & Co., 1957.

Brownson, O.A. *Conversations on Liberalism and the Church*. New York: D & J. Sadlier & Co., 1887.

Works. Vols. I-III (1883), vols. IV,VI (1898), Vols. V- VIII (1884), Ed. H.F. Brownson. Detroit: Thorndike Nourse.

Channing, William Ellery. *Correspondence*. Ed. A.L.L. Breton. Boston: Roberts Brothers, 1874.

Memoir, with Extracts from his Correspondence and Manuscripts. 3 vols. Boston: American Unitarian Association, 1874.

Poems of Sixty-five Years. Ed. F.B. Sanborn. Philadelphia and Concord: James H. Bentley, 1902.

Slavery and Emancipation. New York: Negro Univ. Press, 1836.

Thoreau: the Poet-Naturalist. New York: Biblo & Tannen, 1966.

Works (New and Complete Edition). Boston: American Unitarian Association, 1896.

Clarke, James Freeman. *Autobiography, Diary and Correspondence*. Ed. E.V. Hale. Boston and New York: Houghton Mifflin, 1891.

Everyday Religion. Boston and New York: Houghton, Mifflin, 1893.

Memorial and Biographical Sketches. Boston: Houghton, Osgood, 1878.

Ten Great Religions. Boston: James R. Osgood, 1871.

Conway, Moncure Daniel. *Emerson at Home and Abroad*. Boston: James R. Osgood, 1882.

My Pilgrimage to the Wise Men of the East. Boston and New York: Houghton, Mifflin, 1906.

The Life of Thomas Paine. New York: Benjamin Blom, Inc., 1972.

DIAL: *A Magazine for Literature, Philosophy, and Religion*. 4 Vols. New York: Russell and Russell, 1961.

Emerson, Ralph Waldo. *Complete Works*. 12 vols. Boston & New York: Houghton, Mifflin, 1903.

Journals. 10 vols. Ed. E.W. Emerson and W.E. Forbes. Boston and New York: Houghton, Mifflin, 1909-14.

The Early Lectures. Vol.1., Ed. S.E. Whicher and H.E. Spiller. Mass.: Harvard Univ. Press, 1959.

The Letters of Ralph Waldo Emerson. 6 vols., Ed. R.L. Husk. New York and London: Columbia Univ. Press. 1966.

Frothingham, Octavius Brooks. *George Ripley* Boston: Houghton, Mifflin, 1882.

Transcendentalism in New England: A History. New York: Harper Touchbook, 1959.

Hedge, Frederic Henry. *Atheism in Philosophy and Other Essays*. Boston: Roberts Brothers, 1884.

Higginson, T.W. *Letters and Journals (1846-1906)*. Ed. M.T. Higginson. Boston and New York: Houghton, Mifflin, 1921.

Out-Door Papers. Boston: James R. Osgood, 1874.

Johnson, Samuel. *Oriental Religions and Their Relation to Universal Religion: India*. Boston: James R. Osgood, 1873.

Ossoli, Sarah Margaret (Fuller), *Margaret Fuller: American Romantic: A Selection from her Writings and Correspondence*. Ed. P. Miller. Mass: Peter Smith, 1969.

The Writings of Margaret Fuller. Ed. M. Wade. New York: Viking Press, 1941.

Parker, Theodore. *An Anthology*. Ed. H.S. Commager. Boston: Beacon Press, 1960.

A Sermon of Old Age. Boston: Benjamin B. Mussey & Co., 1854.

Views of Religion. Boston: American Unitarian Association, 1906.

Poets of Transcendentalism: An Anthology. Ed. G.W. Cooke. Boston and New York: Houghton Mifflin, 1903.

Sanborn, F.B. and W.T. Harris. *A Bronson Alcott: His Life and Philosophy*. 2 vols. New York: Biblo and Tannen, 1965.

Ralph Waldo Emerson. Boston: Small, Maynard & Co., 1901.

Thoreau, Henry David. *Writings*. 20 vols. Ed. B. Torrey. New York: Ams Press, 1968.

Transcendentalists an Anthology. Ed. P. Miller. Mass.: Harvard Univ. Press, 1967.

Very, Jones. *Poems*. Ed. W.P. Andrew. Boston: Houghton, Mifflin, 1883.

Poems and Essays. Boston & New York: Houghton, Mifflin, 1886.

Books on Indian Scriptures:

Babbitt, Irving. *The Dhammapada*. New York: New Directions Books, 1965.

Bahm, Archie J. *Philosophy of the Buddha*. New York: Harper and Brothers, 1958.

Select Bibliography

Yoga: Union with the Ultimate (Patanjali's Yoga Sutras). New York: Frederick Ungar Pub. Co., 1961.

Bhatta, Kūlluka. *Manusmṛti*. Varanasi: Chowkhamba, 1970.

Chakravarti, S.C. *The Philosophy of the Upanishads*. Calcutta: Univ. of Cal., 1935.

Chidbhavanand, Swami. *The Bhagavad Gitā*. Madras: Sri Ramkrishna Tapovanam, 1969.

Chinmayanand, Swami. *Talks on Sankara's Vivekachoodamani*. Bombay: Chinmaya Mission Trust, 1977.

Dasgupta, Surendranath. *The History of Indian Philosophy*. 5 vols. Delhi, Motilal Banarasidas, 1975.

Edgerton, F. *The Bhagavad Gitā*. Mass.: Harvard Univ. Press. 1972.

Eliade, Mircea. *Yoga: Immortality and Freedom*. Trans. W.R. Trask. New York: Princeton Univ. Press, 1970.

Gardner, Adelaide. *Meditation: A Practical Study*. Wheaton: Theosophical Pub. House. 1968.

Hiriyanna, M. *Outlines of Indian Philosophy*. London: George Allen & Unwin, 1970.

Isherwood, Christopher. *An Approach to Vedanta*. Hollywood: Vedanta Press. 1963.

Keith, A.B. *The Religion and Philosophy of the Veda and Upanishads* Vol. 32. Cambridge, Mass.: Harvard Univ. Press, 1925.

Law, Narendra Nath. *Age of the Ṛgveda*. Calcutta, Firma K.L. Mukhopadhyay, 1965.

Macdonell, Arthur A.*A History of Sanskrit Literature*. New Delhi, Munshiram Manoharlal, 1972.

Mani, Vetam. *Purāṇic Encyclopaedia*. Delhi, Motilal Banarasidas, 1975.

Murti, T.R.V. *The Central Philosophy of Buddhism: A Study of the Madhyamika System*. London: George Allen & Unwin, 1960.

Nityaswarupananda, Swami. *Astāvakra Saṁhita*. Calcutta: Advaita Ashraṁ, 1975.

Poddar, Hanumanprasad. *The Philosophy of Love: Bhakti-Sutras of Devarsi Nārada*. Rajgangpur: Orissa Cement Ltd.,-.

Prabhavananda, Swami. *Śrimad Bhagavatam*. Madras: Sri Ramkrishna Math.

Radhakrishnan, S. *The Brahma Sūtra: The Philosophy of Spiritual Life*. London: George Allen & Unwin, 1960.

Indian Philosophy. 2 vols. London: George Allen & Unwin, 1966.

The Principal Upanisads. London: George Allen & Unwin, 1968.

Raja, Dr. C. Kunhan. *Poet-Philosophers of the Ṛgveda*. Madras: Ganesh & Co., 1963.

Shrava, Satya. *A Comprehensive History of Vedic Literature: Brahmana & Aranyaka Works*. New Delhi: Pranava Prakashan, 1977.

Select Bibliography

Sircar, Mahendranath. *Hindu Mysticism: According to the Upaniṣads*. New Delhi: Oriental Books Reprint Corporation, 1974.

Vedanta for Modern Man. Ed. C. Isherwood. New York: Collier Books, 1962.

Vedanta for the Western World. Ed. C. Isherwood. London: George Allen & Unwin, 1949.

Vivekananda, Swami. *Jnana Yoga*. Calcutta: Advaita Ashram, 1972.

Williams, Monier. *Indian Wisdom or Examples of the Religions, Philosophical and Ethical Doctrines of the Hindus*. Delhi: Indian Reprint Pub. Co., 1974.

Wilson, H.H. *The Vishṅu Purāṅa*. Calcutta: Punthi Pustak, 1972.

Woods, J.H. *The Yoga-System of Patañjali*. Delhi, Motilal Banarasidass, 1966.

Yatiswarananda, Swami. *Adventures in Vedanta*. London: Rider & Co., 1961.

Secondary Sources:

Ahlstrom, S.E. *A Religious History of the American People*. London: Yale Univ. Press, 1973.

Akhilananda, Swami. *Hindu Psychology: Its Meaning for the West*. London: Routledge & Kegan Paul Ltd., 1948.

Allen, Gay Wilson. *The New Walt Whitman Handbook*. New York: New York Univ. Press, 1975.

The Solitary Singer: A Critical Biography of Walt Whitman. New York: The MacMillan Co., 1955.

Anderson, C.R. *The Magic Circle of Walden*. New York: Holt, Rinehart and Winston, 1968.

Aurobindo, Sri. *The Life Divine*. 2 vols. Calcutta: Arya Publishing House, 1940.

Baird, James. *Ishmael*. Baltimore: Johns Hopkins Press, 1956.

Barbour, B.M. Ed. *American Transcendentalism an Anthology of Criticism*. London: Univ. of Notre Dame Press, 1973.

Barrows, Rev. J. H. *The World's Parliament of Religions*. vol.1. Chicago: Parliament Publishing Co., 1893.

Bartlett, W.I. *Jones Very: Emerson's "Brave Saint*." New York: Greenwood Press, 1968.

Basham, A.L. Ed. *A Cultural History of India*. London: Clarendon Press, 1975.

Benet, W.R. and N.H. Pearson. Ed. *The Oxford Anthology of American Literature*. New York: Oxford Univ. Press, 1963.

Bennett, Charles A. *A Philosophical Study of Mysticism: An Essay*. New Haven: Yale Univ. Press, 1923.

Berry, Edmund Grindley. *Emerson's Plutarch*. Mass.: Harvard Univ. Press, 1961.

Bhagat, G. *Americans in India 1784-1860*. New York: New York Univ. Press, 1970.

Select Bibliography

Bible: Revised Standard Version. London: WM. Collins Sons & Co. 1952.

Bishop, J. *Emerson on the Soul*. Mass.: Harvard Univ. Press, 1964.

Blair, Walter., et al. *The Literature of the United States*. Vol.1. Chicago: Scott. Foresman & Co., 1946.

Bode, Carl. Ed. *The Portable Thoreau*. New York: Viking Press 1974.

Boller, Paul F. *American Transcendentalism, 1830-1860: An Intellectual Inquiry*. New York: G.P. Putnam's Sons, 1974.

Bolster, A. S. *James Freeman Clarke: Disciple to Advancing Truth*. Boston: Beacon Press, 1954.

Brooks, Van Wyck. *The Flowering of New England: 1815-1865*. New York: Modern Library, 1936.

The Life of Emerson. New York: E.P. Dutton Co., 1932.

Brown, A.W. *Margaret Fuller*. Conn.: College & Univ. Press, 1964.

William Ellery Channing. New York: Twayne Pub. Inc., 1962.

Brown, J.W. *The Rise of Biblical Criticism in America, 1800-1870: The New England Scholar*. Conn.: Wesleyan Univ. Press, 1969.

Buell, Lawrence. *Literary Transcendentalism: Style and Vision in the American Renaissance*. New Delhi: Eurasia, 1974.

Burtis, M.E. *Moncure Conway: 1832-1907*. New Jersey: Rutgers Univ. Press, 1952.

Cabot, James Elliot. *A Memoir of Ralph Waldo Emerson*. 2 vols. Boston & New York: Houghton, Mifflin, 1887.

Cambon, G. *Budding America*. Milan-Paris-Rome: Institut Des Hautes Etudes D'Interpretariat,-.

Cameron, K.W. Ed. *Concord Harvest*. 2 vols. Hartford: Transcendental Books, 1970.

Campanion to Thoreau's Correspondence. Hartford: Transcendental Books, 1964.

Contemporary Dimension: An American Literary Notebook. Hartford: Transcendental Books, 1970.

Emerson Among His Contemporaries. Hartford: Transcendental Books, 1967.

Emerson the Essayist. 2 vols. Hartford: Transcendental Books, 1945.

Research Keys to the American Renaissance. Hartford: Transcendental Books, 1967.

Response to Transcendental Concord. Hartford: Transcendental Books, 1974.

Transcendental Climate: New Resources for the Study of Emerson, Thoreau and Their Contemporaries. 3 vols. Hartford: Transcendental Books.

Transcendental Epilogue. Hartford: Transcendental Books, 1965.

Select Bibliography

The Transcendentalists and Minerva. 3 vols. Hartford: Transcendental Books, 1958.

Transcendental Reading Patterns. Hartford: Transcendental Books, 1970.

Whitman, Byrant, Melville and Holmes Among Their Contemporaries. Hartford: Transcendental Books, 1976.

Young Emerson's Transcendental Vision. Hartford: Transcendental Books, 1971.

Conby, H.S. *Thoreau*. Boston: Beacon Press, 1939.

Cannon, Garland. *Oriental Jones*. New York: Asia Pub. House, 1964.

Capra, Fritjot. *The Tao of Physics*. Suffolk Fontana/ Collins, 1978.

Carpenter, Frederic Ives. *Emerson and Asia*. New York: Haskell House, 1968.

Emerson Handbook. New York: Handricks House, 1953.

Cavell, S. *The Senss of Walden*. New York: Viking Press, 1972.

Century Dictionary and Cyclopedia. 12 vols. New York: The Century Co., 1913.

Chandra, L. Ed. *India's Contribution to World Thought and Culture*. Madras: Vivekananda Rock Memorial,-.

Channing, W.H. *The Life of William Ellery Channing*. Boston: American Unitarian Association, 1904.

Chari, V.K. *Whitman in the Light of Vedantic Mysticism: An Interpretation*. Lincoln: Univ. of Nebraska Press, 1964.

Chaudhuri, H. & F. Spiegelberg. Ed. *The Integral Philosophy of Sri Aurobindo*. London:George Allen & Unwin, 1960.

Chevigny, D.G. *The Woman and the Myth: Margaret Fuller's Life and Writings*. New York: Peminist Press, 1976.

Chipperfield, F. *In Quest of Love: The Life and Death of Margaret Fuller*. New York: Coward-McCann, 1957.

Christy, Arthur E. Ed. *The Asian Legacy and American Life*. New York: Greenwood Press, 1968.

The Orient in American Transcendentalism: A Study of Emerson, Thoreau, and Alcot. New York: Octagon Books, 1963.

Clark, H.H. Ed. *Transitions in American Literary History*. Durham: Duke Univ. Press, 1953.

Commager, H.S. *Theodore Parker*. Boston: Little, Brown, & Co. 1936.

Cooke, G.W. *Memorabilia of the Transcendentalists in New England*. 2 vols. Hartfort: Transcendental Books, 1973.

Cowley, M. Ed. *Introduction to Walt Whitman's Leaves of Grass: The First (1855) Edition*. New York: Viking Press, 1967.

Crawford, B.V. *Henry David Thoreau*. New York: American Book Co., 1934.

Crowe, Charles. *George Ripley: Transcendentalist and Utopian Socialist*. Athens, Univ. of Georgia Press, 1967.

Curti, Merle. *The Growth of American Thought*. New Delhi: Tata McGraw-Hill, 1964.

Das, S.P."Emerson's Debt to Hindu Thought: A Reappraisal". Diss. Gurunanak Dev Univ. Amritsar, 1977.

Dennis, Carld Edward. "The Poetry of Mind and Nature: A Study of the Idea of Nature in American Transcendental Poetry." Diss. Microfilm Copy (positive) of type script. Univ. of California, Berkely, 1966.

Deshmukh, D.G. *Thoreau and Indian Thought: A Study of the Impact of Indian Thought on the Life and Writings of Henry David Thoreau*. Nagpur: Nagpur Univ., 1974.

Detweiler, Robert. "Emerson's Concept of God." Diss. Univ. of Florida, 1962.

Dictionary of the History of Ideas. Vol.III. Ed. Philip P. Wiener. New York: Charles Scribner's, 1973.

Dillaway, Newton. *Prophet of America: Emerson and the Problems of To-day*. Boston: Little, Brown, & Co., 1936.

Dirks, J.E. *The Critical Theology of Theodore Parker*. New York: Columbia Univ. Press, 1948.

Duncan, J.L. *The Power and Form of Emerson's Thought*. Charlottesville: Univ. Press of Virginia, 1973.

Dwivedi, A.N. *Thoreau: A Study*. Bareilly: Prakash Book, 1974.

Eddy, M.B. *Science and Health*. Boston: First Church of Christ, 1971.

Elder, J.W. *Chapters in Indian Civilization*. vol.II. Wisconsin: Univ. of Wisconsin, 1967.

Encyclopaedia of Religion. Ed. V. Form. New York: Philosophical Library, 1945.

Encyclopaedia of Religion and Ethics. Ed. J. Hastings. Edinburgh: T & T Clark, 1961.

Feidelson, C.& P. Brodtkorb. Ed. *Interpretations of American Literature*. New York: Oxford Univ. Press, 1967.

Feidelson, C. *Symbolism and American Literature*. Chicago, Univ. of Chicago Press, 1953.

Forbes, J.D. Ed. *The Indian in America's Past*. Englewood Cliffs: Prentice-Hall, 1964.

Foster, F.H. *A Genetic History of the New England Theology*. New York: Russell and Russell, 1963.

Foy, R.L.W. "The Philosophy of Ralph Waldo Emerson and its Educational Implications." Diss. Univ. of Texas, 1962.

Gandhi, Mahatma. *Collected Works*. 30 volumes. Delhi: Publications Division, 1962-66.

Garnett, R. *Life of Ralph Waldo Emerson*. London: Walter Scott, 1888.

Gittleman, E. *Jones Very: The Effective Years 1833-1840*. New York: Columbia Univ. Press, 1967.

Ed. *The Minor and Later Transcendentalists: A Symposium.* Hartford: Transcendental Books, 1969.

Golemba, H.L. *George Ripley.* Boston: Twayne Publishers, 1977.

Gottschalk, S. *The Emergence of Christian Science in American Religious Life.* Los Angels: Univ. of California Press, 1974.

Gould, James Warren. *The First American Contact with Asia.* Calif.: Society for Oriental Studies, 1960.

Gray, H.D. *Emerson: A Statement of New England Transcendentalism as Expressed in the Philosophy of its Chief Exponent.* New York: Frederick Ungar Pub. Co., 1965.

Harding, Walter. *A Thoreau Handbook.* New York: New York Univ. Press, 1959.

The Days of Henry Thoreau. New York: Alfred 'A' Knoph, 1966.

Ed. *Thoreau: A Century of Criticism.* Dallas: Southern Methodist Univ. Press, 1954.

Harrison, J.S. *The Teachers of Emerson.* New York: Haskell House, 1966.

Higginson, M.T. *Thomas Wentworth Higginson:The Study of His Life.* Boston & New York: Houghton, Mifflin, 1914.

Howe, Julia. *Margaret Fuller.* Conn.: Greenwood Press. 1970.

Hutchison, William R. *The Transcendental Ministers: Church Reform in the New England Renaissance.* Boston: Beacon Press, 1965.

Huxley, Aldous. *The Perennial Philosophy*. London: Chatto & Windus, 1947.

James, W. *The Varieties of Religious Experience*. New York: Modern Library, 1902.

Jones, Howard Humford. *Belief and Disbelief in American Literature*. Chicago: Univ. of Chicago Press, 1967.

Josi, K.N. *The West Looks at India*. Bareilly: Prakash Book 1969.

Kamath, M.V. *The United States and India 1776-1976*. Washington: Embassy of India, 1976.

Kant, Immanuel. *Critique of Pure Reason*. tr. N.K. Smith. New York: Macmillan, 1968.

Karabatsos, James. *A Word-Index to A Week on the Concord and Merrimack Rivers*. Hartford: Transcendental Books, 1971.

Konvitz, M.R. Ed. *The Recognition of Ralph Waldo Emerson: Selected Criticism Since 1837*. Machigan: Univ. of Machigan Press, 1972.

Konvitz, Milton and S. Whicher. *Twentieth Century Views: Emerson: A Collection of Critical Essays*. N.J.: Prentice- Hall, Inc., 1962.

Koster, D.N. *Transcendentalism in America*. Boston: Twayne Pub., 1975.

Kulkarni, H.B. *Moby Dick: A Hindu Avtar: A Study of Hindu Myth and Thought*. Logan: Utah State Univ. Press, 1970.

Lal, Chaman. *Hindu America*. Delhi, Chaman Lal, 1966.

Lapati, A.D. *Orestes A. Brownson*. Conn.: Twayne Pub. Inc., 1965.

Lavan, Spencer. *Unitarians and India: A Study in Encounter and Response*. Boston: Beacon Press, 1977.

Leighton, Walter L. *French Philosophers and New-England Transcendentalism*. New York: Greenwood Press, 1968.

Levin, David. Ed. *Emerson: Prophecy, Metamorphosis and Influence*. New York: Columbia Univ. Press, 1975.

Majumdar, J.K. Ed. *Raja Rammohan Roy and Progressive Movements in India*. Calcutta: Art Press, 1941.

Manchandra,M.K. *India and America: Historical Links 1776-1920*. Chandigarh: Young Men Harmilap Association, 1976.

Matthiessen, F.O. *American Renaissance*. Delhi: Oxford Univ. Press, 1973.

Mc Alean, John J. Ed. *Artist and Citizen Thoreau*. Hartford: Transcendental Books, 1971.

Menen, Aubrey. *The New Mystics and the True Indian Tradition*. London: Thomas & Hudson, 1974.

Mercer, Dorothy F. "Leaves of Grass and the Bhagavad Gita: A Comparative Study." Diss. Univ. of California, 1933.

Miller, F. Dewolfe. *Christopher Pearce Cranch: And His Caricatures of New England Transcendentalism*. Mass.: Harvard Univ. Press, 1951.

Moore, Adrionne. *Rammohun Roy and America*. Calcutta: Brahmo Mission Press, 1942.

Morison, S.E. *Maritime History of Massachusetts, 1783-1860*. Boston: Houghton, Mifflin, 1921.

Mott, F.L. *A History of American Magazines 1741-1850*. Mass.: Belknap Press of Harvard Univ. Press, 1957.

Mukerjee, Radhakamal. *The Theory and Art of Mysticism*. Bombay: Asia Pub. House, 1960.

Melville, Herman. *Moby Dick*. New York: Harper & Brothers, 1950.

Nambiar, O.K. *Maha Yogi Walt Whitman: New Light on Yoga*. Bangalore: Jeevan Pub., 1978.

Narasimhaiah, C.D. Ed. *Asian Response to American Literature*. Delhi: Vikas Publications, 1972.

Ed. *Indian Response to American Literature*. Delhi:Vikas Pub., 1972.

Nölle, Wilfried. *Germany-Veda's Second Home*. Bonn: Bonner Univ., 1965.

Norton, Andrews. *A Discourse on the Latest Form of Infidelity*. Cambridge: Published by John Owen, 1839.

Organ, Troy Wilson. *The Hindu Quest for the Perfection of Men*. Athens: Ohio Univ. Press, 1970.

Western Approaches to Eastern Philosophy. Athens Ohio Univ. Press, 1975.

Otto, Rudolf. *Mysticism East and West*. tr. B.L. Bracey and R.C.Payne. New York:Macmillan, 1972.

Paramananda, Swami. *Emerson and Vedanta*. Boston: Vedanta Centre, 1918.

Pathak, S.M. *American Missionaries and Hinduism*. Delhi, Munshiram Manoharlal, 1967.

Patterson, R.L. *The Philosophy of William Ellery Channing*. New York: Bookman Associates, 1952.

Paul, Sherman. *The Shores of America: Thoreau's Inward Explorations*. New York: Russell & Russell, 1971.

Ed. *Twentieth Century Views: Thoreau: A Collection of Critical Essays*. N.J.: Prentice-Hall, 1962.

Peel, Robert. *Mary Baker Eddy*. New York, Chicago, San Franciscoi: Holt, Hinehart & Winston, 1974.

Plato. *The Dialogues*. tr. B. Jowett. Chicago: Encyclopaedia Britanica, Inc., 1952.

Poe, Edgar Allen. *The Works*. Ed. E. Markham. New York and London: Funk & Wagnalls, 1904.

Porte, Joel. *Representative Man: Ralph Waldo Emerson in His Time*. New York: Oxford Univ. Press, 1979.

Prasad, P.C. *Foreign Trade and Commerce in Ancient India*. New Delhi: Abhinav Publications, 1977.

Radhakrishnan, S. *Eastern Religions and Western Thought*. London: Oxford Univ. Press, 1940.

Rajasekharaiah, T.R. *The Roots of Whitman's Grass*. N. J.: Fairleigh Dickinson Univ., 1970.

Ramakrishna Rao, Adapa. "Emerson's Attitude Toward Humanitarian Reform." Diss. Univ. of Wisconsin, 1964.

Emerson and Social Reform. New Delhi: Arnold-Heinemann, 1980.

Rayapati, J.P.R. *Early American Interest in Vedanta*. Bombay: Asia Pub. House, 1973.

Regan, E.M. *A Literary Introduction to Emerson's Nature*. Hartford: Transcendental Books, 1976.

Reid, John T. *Indian Influences in American Literature and Thought*. New Delhi: Indian Council for Cultural Relations, 1965.

Riley, W. *American Thought from Puritanism to Pragmaticism and Beyond*. Mass.: Peter Smith, 1959.

Roer, E. *Bibliotheca Indica* (A Collection of Oriental Works). Calcutta: East India Co., 1853.

Roszak, T. *The Making of Counter Culture*. New York: Doubleday & Co., 1969.

Rusk, R.L. *The Life of Ralph Waldo Emerson*. New York: Charles Scribner's, 1949.

Sargent, J.T. *Sketches and Reminiscences of the Radical Club of Chestnut Street Boston*. Boston: James H. Osgood, 1880.

Select Bibliography

Schneider, H.W. *The History of American Philosophy*. New York: Columbia Univ. Press, 1947.

Schweitzer, Albert. *Indian Thought and its Development*. tr. C.E.D. Russell. London: Adam Charles Black, 1951.

Shepard, Odell. *Pedlar's Progress: The Life of Bronson Alcott* Boston: Little, Brown & Co., 1937.

Sterwin, J.S. & R.C. Reynolds. *A Word Index to Walden with Textual Notes*. Hartford: Emerson Society, 1969.

Singh, Man Mohan. "Emerson and India." Dis. Univ. of Pennsylvania, 1946.

Stace, W.T. *Mysticism and Philosophy*. Philadelphia & New York: J.B. Lippincott Co., 1960.

Suzuki, D.T. *Mysticism: Christian and Buddhist*. New York: Harper & Brothers, 1957.

Swayne, J.L. Ed. *The Story of Concord: As Told by Concord Writers*. Boston: W.B. Clarke Co., 1911.

Swift, L. *Brook Farm: Its Members, Scholars, and Visitors*. New York: Macmillan, 1900.

Trent, W.P. et.al., *The Cambridge History of American Literature*. 3 Vols. New York: Macmillan, 1954.

Tytell, John. *Naked Angels: The Lives and Literature of the Beat Generation*. New York: McGraw-Hill, 1976.

Van Doren, Mark. *Henry David Thoreau: A Critical Study* Boston: Houghton, Mifflin, 1916.

Watts, Alan W. *Psychotherapy East and West*. London: Jonathan Cape, 1971.

Whicher, G.F. Ed. *The Transcendentalist Revolt*. Mass.:D.C. Heath & Co., 1968.

Whicher, S.E. Ed. *Selections from Ralph Waldo Emerson: An Organic Anthology*. Boston: Houghton Mifflin, 1960.

White, Morton. *Documents in the History of American Philosophy: From Jonathan Edwards to John Dewey*. New York: Oxford Univ. Press, 1972.

Whitman, S.H. *Edgar Poe and His Critics*. New York: Rudd & Carleton, 1860.

Whitman, Walt. *Leaves of Grass*. Philadelphia: David McKay, 1888.

Whittemore, Robert C. *Makers of the American Mind*. New York: William Morrow & Co., 1964.

Whittier, John Green Leaf. *The Letters*. Ed. J.B. Pickard. 3 vols. Mass.: Belknap Press of Harvard Univ. Press, 1975.

Works. 7 vols. Boston and New York: Houghton, Mifflin, 1891.

Woodcock, George. *The Greeks in India*. London: Faber and Faber, 1866.

Articles:

Adams, R.P. "Romanticism and the American Renaissance". *American Literature*, 23 (1951-52), 419-432.

"Emerson and the Organic Metaphor:. *PMLA*, LXIX (March, 1954), 117-130.

Agrawal, I.N. "Whitmann, Twain and Kipling in India: A Study of Experiments in Perspectives." *Univ. of Allahabad Studies*, (July, 1972) 131-140.

Ahlstrom, S.W. "The Interpretation of Channing". *New England Quarterly*, 30, I (March 1957), 99-105.

Bahm, Archie J. "Organicism: The Philosophy of Interdependence." *International Philosophy Quarterly*, VII. 2 (June, 1967), 251-284.

Barnes, Walter R. "The Influence of Emerson." *The Dial*, III, 26 (June, 1882), 25-27.

Bhattacharya, Kalidas. "Classical Philosophies of India and the West." *Philosophy East and West*, VIII, 1-2(April, July,1958) 17-36.

Blackwell, Louise. "'Song of Myself' and the organic Theory of Poetry." *Walt Whitmen Review*, XII, 2 (June, 1966), 35-41.

Blair, Walter and Clarence Frust. "Emerson's Literary Method." *Modern Philology*, 42 (Nov., 1944), 79-95.

Bridman, Richard. "The Meaning of Emerson's Title 'Hamatreya'." *Emerson Society Quarterly*, 27 (II Qrt., 1962), 16.

Broderick, John C. "Bronson Alcott's 'Concord Book'." *New England Quarterly*, 29, 3 (Sept., 1956), 365-80.

"Emerson, Thoreau, and Transcendentalism." *American Literary Scholarship*, (1970), 3-17.

"Imagery in Walden." *Texas Univ. Studies in English*, 32 (1954), 80-89.

Burtt, E.A. 'What can Western Philosophy Learn from India." *Philosophy East and West*, V, 3 (Oct., 1955), 195-210.

Cameron, K.W. "A Historical Introduction: The Rise of Transcendentalism." *ESQ*, 64 & 65 (Summer & Fall, 1971), 7-11.

"A Hymn to Narayana." *American Transcendental Quarterly*, I, 20 (Fall, 1973), 578-83.

"Emerson's Orientalism at Harvard." *ESQ*, 32 (III Qtr., 1963).

"Indian Superstition: By Ralph Waldo Emerson." *ESQ*, 32, I (III Qtr., 1963), 2-35.

"More Background for Emerson's Indian Superstition - Parish Circulating Libraries." *ESQ*, 47 (II Qtr., 1967), 130-138.

"More Notes on Orientalism in Emerson's Harvard." *ESQ*, 22 (I Qtr., 1961), 81-90.

"Sources for Emerson's Early Orientalism." *ESQ*, 64 & 65 (Summer & Fall, 1971), 578-83.

Carpenter, F.I. "American Transcendentalism in India (1961)." *ESQ*, 31 (II Qtr., 1963) 59-62.

"Immortality from India." *American Literature*, I (1929- 1930), 231-42.

Chandrasekharan, K.R. "Emerson's *Brahma*: An Indian Interpretation." *New England Quarterly*, XXXIII, 4 (Dec., 1960), 506-512.

Chari, V.K. "Whitman and Indian Thought." *Western Humanities Review*, 13, 3 (Summer, 1959), 291-302.

Chaudhuri, H. "The Concept of Brahman in Hindu Philosophy." *Philosophy East and West*, IV, I (April, 1954), 47-66.

Christy, A. "Orientalism in New England: Whittier." *AL*, I (1929-30), 372-92.

"The Orientalism of Whittier". *AL*, 5 (1933-34), 247-57.

Conger, George P. "Ancient India and Greece: A Report of an Investigation in Progress." *Indian Philosophical Congress Silver Jubilee Commemoration*, II (1950), 20-26.

"Did India Influence Early Greek Philosophies?" *Philosophy East and West*, (April, 1952), 102-28.

Coomer, M.M. "Ram Doolal Dey: Pioneer of Indo-American Trade." *Span*, Nov., 1976), 42-43.

Detweiler, Robert. "Emerson and Zen." *American Quarterly*, XIV, 3 (Fall, 1962), 422-38.

"The Over-Rated 'Over-Soul'." *AL*, 36, I (March, 1964), 65- 68.

Eisenberg, Philip, "Henry David Thoreau:Apostle of Non-conformity." *Span*, (April, 1969), 12-17.

Fairburn, William A. "The Indian Trade." *Merchant Sail*, 4, 21 (1945-55), 2462-2604.

Frost, Robert. "On Emerson." *Daedalus*, (Fall, 1959), 712- 718.

Furber, H. "The Beginning of American Trade with India, 1784- 1812." *New England Quarterly*, XI (June, 1938) 235-265.

"Historical and Cultural Aspects of Indo-American Relations." *Journal of the Univ. of Bombay*, (July 1965- January, 1966), 45-116.

Gardine, Walter. "Asiatic Influences on Pre-Columbian Cultures." *Diogenes*, 87 (Fall, 1974), 106-25.

Goren, Leyla. "Elements of Brahminism in the Transcendentalism of Emerson." *ESQ*. 34 (I Qtr., 1964), 1-69.

Harding, W. "Emerson, Thoreau and Transcendentalism." *American Literary Scholarship*, (1963), 3-16.

Hendrick, G. "Emerson and Gandhi." *ESQ*, 2 (I Qtr., 1956), 7-8.

Henley, W. "Geologist Thinks Walden Pond Born Almost as Indians Thought." *ESQ*, 3 (II Qtr., 1956), 11-12.

Herbold, A. "Nature as Concept and Technique in the Poetry of Jones Very." *NEQ*, 2 (June, 1967), 244-59.

Higginson, T.W. "Water-Lilies." *Atlantic Monthly*, II, XI (Sept., 1858), 465-73.

Hoch, David G. "Thoreau's Use of the Hindoos." *Thoreau Society Bulletin*, 114 (Winter, 1971), 1-2.

Isani, M.A. "Cotton Mather and the Orient." *NEQ*, 43 (March, 1970), 46-58.

Kennedy, W.S. "Clews to Emerson's Mystic Verse." *American Transcendental Quarterly*, 3 (Winter, 1976), 2-20.

Kim, Kichung. "Thoreau's Science and Teleology." *ESQ*, 18, 3 (III Qtr., 1972), 125-33.

Le, Van-Diem. "Puritan Idealism and Transcendental Movement." *Dissertation Abstracts*, XXI (1961), 1929.

Lee, Ronald F. "Emerson's 'Compensation' as Argument and as Art." *New England Quarterly*, 37, 3 (Sept., 1964), 291-305.

Leidecker, Kurt F. "Emerson and East-West Synthesis." *Philosophy East and West*, 1,2 (July, 1951), 40-50.

Levenson, J.C. "Christopher Pearse Cranch: The Case History of a Minor Artist in America." *AL*, 21 (1949-50), 415-26.

Levernier, James A. "Calvinism and Transcendentalism in the Poetry of Jones Very." *ESQ*, 24, 1 (1 Qtr., 1978), 30-41.

MacShane, Frank. "Walden and Yoga." *New England Quarterly*, XXXVII, 3 (Sept., 1964), 322-342.

Malloy, Charles. "A Study of Emerson's Major Poems". (BRAHMA) *ATQ*, I (Summer, 1974), 60-66.

Marlow, A.N. "Hinduism and Buddhism in Greek Philosophy." *Philosophy East and West*, (April, 1954), 35-45.

Mehta, Usha. "Gandhi, Thoreau and Green".' *Journal of the Univ. of Bombay*, I 4 (July 1963-January 1964), 19-26.

Mellow, James R. 'Brook Farm: An American Utopia.' "American Review", 24, 4 (Summer, 1980), 44-52.

Mueller, Roger Chester. "The Orient in American Transcendental Periodicals (1835-1886)." *DA*, 29, 8 (Feb., 1969), 2681-A.

"A Significant Buddhist Translation by Thoreau." *Thoreau Society Bulletin*, 138 (Winter, 1977), 1-2.

Munz, Peter. "Basic Intuitions of East and West." *PEW*, V, I (April, 1955), 43-56.

"Indian and the West: A Synthesis." *PEW*, V, 4 (January 1956), 321-38.

"Relationship and Solitude in Hinduism and Christianity." *PEW*, VI, 2 (July, 1956), 137-52.

Myerson, Jool. "In the Transcendental Emporium: Bronson Alcott's 'Orphic Sayings' in the Dial." *English Language Notes*, X, I (Sept., 1972), 31-38.

"Memoranda and Documents: Two Unpublished Reminiscences of Brook Farm." *NEQ*, XLVIII, 2 (June, 1975), 253-60.

Nagley, W.E. "Thoreau on Attachment, Detachment, and Non- Attachment." *PEW*, III, 4 (January, 1954), 307-20.

Nelson, Carl. "The Rhetoric of Emerson's Hindu 'Heroism'." *ESQ*, 18, 4 (IV Qtr., 1972), 258-64.

Oliver, E.S. "The Brahmins did not know India." *Univ. of Kansas City Review*, (Winter, 1959), 129-32.

Organ, T.W. 'The Silence of the Buddha.' "PEW", IV, 2 (July, 1954), 125-40.

Parker, Theodore. 'The Revival of Religion which We Need: A Sermon, Delivered at Music Hall, Boston, on Sunday, April 11, 1858.' "ESQ", 59 (Spring, 1970), 87-94.

Parsons, Theophilus. "Manners and Customs of India." *North American Review*, IX (1819), 36-58.

Passmore, John. "Paradise Now: The Logic of the New Mysticism." *Encounter*, (Nov., 1970), 3-21.

Paul, Sherman. "The Wise Silence: Sound as the Agency of Correspondence in Thoreau." *NEQ*, XXII, 4 (Dec., 1949), 511- 27.

Paulists, Brother F. Joseph. "Emerson's Concept of Good and Evil." *DA*, XV (1955), 1063-64.

Potter, Charles Francis. "The Hindu Invasion of America." *Modern Thinker and Author's Review*, I, I (March, 1932), 16-23.

Quinn, P.F. "Emerson and Mysticism." *AL*, XXI (January, 1950), 397-414.

"Poe's Eureka and Emerson's Nature." *ESQ*, 31 (11 Qtr., 1963), 4-7.

Raju, P.T. "Idealisms: Eastern and Western." *PEW*, V, 3, 211-34.

Ramakrishna, D. "Poe's Eureka and Hindu Philosophy." *ESQ*, 47, I (II Qtr., 1967), 28-32.

Reaver, J.R. "Mythology in Emerson's Poem." *ESQ*, 39, 2 (1965), 56-63.

Riepe, Dale. "The Indian Influence in American Philosophy: Emerson to Moore." *PEW*, 17, 1-4 (Jan.-Oct., 1967), 125-137.

Ross, Donald. "Emerson's 'Brahma'." *ESQ*, 39, II (II Qtr., 1965), 42-43.

Sanborn, F.B. "Collected Poems of Franklin Benjamin Sanborn of Transcendental Concord." Ed. J.M. Moran. *ESQ*, 40 (III Qtr., 1965), 1-49.

"Emerson Among the Poets." *ATQ*, II (Spring, 1977, 66-67.

"The Emerson-Thoreau Correspondence." *Atlantic Monthly*, 69 (May & June, 1892), 577-596, 737-753.

Schmidt, N. "Essay on Emerson and Oriental Thought." *ESQ*, 21 (IV Qtr., 1960), 39-41.

Schneider, R.J. "*Cape Code*: Thoreau's Wilderness of Illusion." *ESQ*, 26, 4 (IV Qtr., 1980), 184-196.

Schultz, Arthur A. and H.A. Pochmann. "George Ripley: Unitarian Transcendentalist, or Infidel?" *AL*, 14 (1942-43), 1-19.

Singh, R.K. "Whitman: Avatar of Shri Krishna?" *Walt Whitman Review*, 15, 2. (June, 1969), 97-102.

Smithlin, Arnold. "*Eureka*: Poe as Transcendentalist." *ESQ*, 39, II (II Qtr., 1965), 25-28.

"Henry Miller and the Transcendental Spirit." *ESQ*, 43, 2 (II Qtr., 1966), 50-56.

Stein, W.B. "A Bibliography of Hindu and Buddhist Literature Available to Thoreau Through 1854." *ESQ*, 47, II (II Qtr., 1967), 52-56.

"The Hindu Matrix of *Walden*: The King's Son." *Comparative Literature*, XXII, 3 (Summer, 1970), 303-318.

"Thoreau's First Book: A Spoor of Yoga: The Orient in a Week on the Concord and Merrimack Rivers." *ESQ*, 41 (IV Qtr., 1965), 4-25.

Stoller, Leo. "Thoreau's Doctrine of Simplicity." *NEQ*, XXIX, 4 (Dec., 1956), 443-461.

Strauch, Carl F. "The Sources of Emerson's 'Song of Nature'." *Harvard Library Bulletin*, IX (Autumn 1955), 300-334.

"Emerson's Sacred Science." *PMLA*, LXXIII, 3 (June, 1958), 237-250.

Tudor, William. "Theology of the Hindoos as Taught by Ram Mohan Ray." *North American Review*, VI (1817-1818), 386-393.

Washburn, W.E. "The Oriental 'Roots' of American Transcendentalism." *Southwestern Journal*, IV, 4 (Fall, 1949), 141-55.

Weiss, Paul. "The Gita: East and West." *PEW*, IV, 3 (Oct., 1954), 253-58.

Wermuth, P.C. "Santayana and Emerson." *ESQ*, 31 (II Qtr., 1963), 36-40.

White, Robert L. "BRAHMA". *Explicator*, XXI, 8 (April, 1963), Item 63.

Wilkins, Charles. "The Bhagavat-Geeta, or Dialogues of Krishna Arjoon: in Eighteen Lectures; with Notes." *ATQ*, I, 20 (Fall, 1973), 156pp.

Willson, Lawrence. "The Gods of New England." *Specific Spectator*, 9, 2 (Spring, 1955), 141-53.

Woodruff, S.C. "Emerson's 'Self-Reliance' and 'Experience': A Comparison." *ESQ*, 47 (II Qtr., 1967), 48-50.

Writaker, Thomas R. "The Riddle of Emerson's 'Spbinx'." *AL*, 27 (May, 1955), 179-195.

INDEX

Index

Index